CANADA
FROM EH TO ZED

Book Two: Places

CANADA FROM EH TO ZED

Book Two: Places

IN CANADA

IN THE UNITED STATES

FB Productions
Box 408
Virgil, Ontario
L0S 1T0

FB Productions
Box 1297
Lewiston, New York 14092-8297

Canadian Cataloguing in Publication Data

DeRocco, David, 1961-
Canada from eh to zed

Contents: Bk. 2. Places.
ISBN 1-895451-13-2 (bk. 2)

1. Readers - Canada - Miscellanea. 2. English
language - Textbooks for second language learners.*
3. Canada - Miscellanea. I. Chabot, John F.,
1959- . II. Title.

PE1128.D47 1995   428.6'4   C95-930170-4

Illustrations: Christine Porter
Series Editor: John Sivell

ISBN 1-895451-13-2

INTRODUCTION

CANADA FROM EH TO ZED is a reproducible ESL/EFL reading-and-discussion text for false beginners, or for the true beginners who have already had about eight months of instruction in the language. It offers a number of important design features to make both teaching and learning easier and more enjoyable.

1) Contextualized learning: The short self-contained articles in each unit benefit from a very clear focus that facilitates realistic concentration on inter-related items of vocabulary and grammar that are relevant to the topic and the argumentative purpose.

2) Content that really matters: Each unit examines an element of the Canadian experience that will genuinely interest and inform not only immigrants to this nation but also learners abroad who want to know more about the history, geography and culture of Canada. Francophone students in this country will benefit from the opportunity to practice the language through readings that link with their own background knowledge.

3) Lively journalistic style: Although the passages are carefully limited to an elementary level of language difficulty, their style remains vivid and authentic. Readers will be enchanted by the beauty of "Lake Louise", fascinated by the story of "Manitoulin Island", and awed by the power of the tides at the "Bay of Fundy".

4) Well-balanced exercises: The plentiful exercises offer a good range of integrated activities for each unit -- getting the main idea, basic comprehension, finding details, inferences, interpretation and extension of important concepts, vocabulary study, a word puzzle, and a cloze exercise.

5) Illustrations: There is a clear and evocative illustration in each unit; this can be used as a pre-reading exercise, for vocabulary brainstorming, or as the basis for discussion.

6) Answer Key: The text includes a full answer key for every closed-ended question in every unit.

7) Reproducible: Purchase of a copy of the text brings explicit permission to reproduce pages at will, for the use of students at the site where the text is kept.

This package can be used quite simply as it is presented in these pages. In fact, it was carefully planned to be effective in that way. However, resourceful teachers will most likely want to consider one or more of the following suggestions:

- Pre-Activity: Instead of immediately beginning to read the passage, have students start with a discussion or game to encourage thought about the theme or content of the unit. The picture or title at the head of the unit can be useful in this connection; so can newspaper or magazine illustrations or headlines, or current television or radio news items.

- Order of Exercises: By all means, use all the activities provided for each unit, and allow sufficient time for these to be completed thoroughly (including time for small groups to discuss alternate answers and so on). But build in variety by changing the order in which the exercises are done, and by varying the designation of activities for in-class or at-home assignment.

- Intensity of Work: Be sure to take full advantage of the wide range of different kinds of involvement that these materials offer. At one end of the continuum, for instance, the Interpretation questions can be used to inspire free, creative discussion of themes, values and general ideas. By contrast, at the other end of the continuum, the Word Power exercises provide an excellent foundation for practice in all the detailed and demanding but very important strategies for independent vocabulary development: not just careful contextual reading and word-part analysis, but also dictionary and thesaurus use. Resourceful attention to this kind of varied involvement with the materials will make teaching and learning more enjoyable and more effective, too.

- Post-Activity: Once the class has finished the set of exercises in the text itself, think about rounding off the cycle with a post-activity that clearly links the book and the schoolroom to the wider world. Learners might pursue the theme or content of a given unit by making a bulletin-board collage of their own art work and/or comments, writing letters to a relevant person or institution, going on a visit, watching a video...you will find many ways to reinforce the vocabulary, grammar and content one more time while you also build the self-image of learners as competent language-users for real-life purposes.

- Flexibility: There is no problem with using these units in alphabetical order, just as provided, but in many circumstances their best application will be as a flexible data-base of content-centred readings that you can access as you see fit, to tap into the energy of learners' natural curiosity about such passing interests as news items, current movies, new music, or extra-curricular activities. Dip into this treasure-trove of self-contained units to find the exact passage to exploit a "hot topic." Each term, you'll have different students with different experiences, and so your use of the text will differ as well. With this flexible resource, you can change to meet your students' needs!

John Sivell

A: Atlantic Provinces

1   At just over 128 years old, Canada is considered a young country in comparison to the other great nations of the world. And while much of its early history was spent "growing up" in Ontario and Quebec, there's no question that Canada was "born" in the Atlantic Provinces.

2   Due to its coastal location, the entire region known as the Atlantic Provinces of Canada became a gateway to the new continent. From the time Viking explorer Leif Erikson first landed on Canada's eastern seaboard in the 11th century, the area served as a starting point for countless journeys made by travellers heading westward across the unexplored lands of North America.

3   Canada's Atlantic Provinces include the three Maritime Provinces of Prince Edward Island, Nova Scotia and New Brunswick, along with the Province of Newfoundland, which includes Labrador. These Maritime provinces share a great deal of culture and history dating back to Canada's birth as a nation, although Newfoundland remained independent until finally joining Canada in 1949.

4   In total, these four provinces occupy an area of 275,480 square kilometres, less than three per cent of the land mass of the entire country and one-fifth the size of Ontario. However, the provinces are spread over a very large area. In fact, the distance from the eastern-most part of Newfoundland to the northwestern boundary of New Brunswick measures nearly 1,300

kilometres. This is about the same distance travelled on a flight between Toronto and Halifax.

5   Despite the relatively small size of the provinces, they played an important role in the ever-expanding interests of the French and English in Canada from the time such settlers first arrived from Europe. In fact, the Atlantic Provinces were a battle-zone for many of the earliest North American conflicts between France and Britain.

6   Although French explorer Jacques Cartier had visited Canada's Atlantic coast as early as 1534, it was the English under Sir Humphry Gilbert who in 1583 first claimed possession of what is now Newfoundland. The French were the first to build permanent settlements in the three Maritime Provinces, beginning with Nova Scotia in 1605.

7   Both France and England continued to make claims on the land until 1756, when the Seven Years War broke out between the two countries. When the war finally ended in 1763, England was awarded sole ownership of the entire region.

8   Although the Atlantic Provinces are often grouped together, each province has its own distinct character. Newfoundland, the largest of the four, lists fishing as its major industry, and many Newfoundlanders share a strong bond with the sea. New Brunswick, with its striking landscape of farms and forests, is nicknamed the "Picture Province" for its beautiful scenery. Halifax, the capital of Nova Scotia, is the largest city in Eastern Canada, while Prince Edward Island, Canada's smallest province, is also known as the setting for the Anne of Green Gables novels.

9   Despite their small geography, the Atlantic Provinces play a *big* part in Canada's overall personality.

THE MAIN IDEA

Circle the letter of the sentence which best describes the main idea of the article about the Atlantic Provinces. Be prepared to support your answer.

a) The birth of a nation
b) The early claims to the Atlantic Provinces.
c) The history, size and importance of the four smallest provinces.
d) The geography of the Atlantic Provinces.

UNDERSTANDING WHAT YOU READ

If you can, answer these questions from memory. If you cannot, look back at the article.

1) What are the names of the Atlantic Provinces?

2) What is the distance between the eastern-most part of Newfoundland and the northwestern boundary of New Brunswick? About how far is that?

3) Who were the first to build permanent settlements in the three Maritime Provinces? When and where did they start?

4) Name something that gives each of the four provinces a distinct character?

REMEMBERING DETAILS

Write TRUE or FALSE under each statement. If the statement is false, write the statement correctly.

1) Newfoundland remained independent until it joined Canada in 1949.

2) The Atlantic Provinces make up over fifty percent of Canada's land mass.

3) Ever since they arrived here, the French and English have lived peacefully, side by side in the Atlantic Provinces.

4) The Atlantic Provinces add nothing to Canada because they are too small.

INFERENCES

Based on the article, circle the letter of the best sentence completion.

1) The Atlantic Provinces have been called a gateway to North America because...

a) they do not take up a great deal of space.
b) there are cliffs on either side of the Halifax harbour that resemble a gate.
c) early explorers had to travel through them to get to the interior of the continent.
d) Leif Erikson named it that.

2) The Atlantic Provinces are so important to Canada because....

a) Canadians would be cut off from the sea without them.
b) each one has something distinct to add to the makeup of Canada.
c) all the best hockey players come from the east coast.
d) the French and English fought so hard to keep the Americans from taking over.

INTERPRETATION

1) What does the writer mean when he says that "...while much of its early history was spent "growing up" in Ontario and Quebec, there's no question that Canada was "born" in the Atlantic Provinces?"

2) List the Canada's ten provinces and something distinct about each one.

3) Research and prepare a short presentation about one of the Atlantic Provinces. If you like, you can concentrate on one aspect of the province. Aspects can include things like the province's industry, history, geography, etc.

WORD POWER

Circle the letter of the word that means the same as the word on the left.

1) gateway	a) drawback	b) conclusion	c) doorway
2) countless	a) lengthy	b) many	c) meaningless
3) occupy	a) space	b) fill	c) claim
4) relative	a) comparative	b) magnificent	c) growing
5) broke out	a) started	b) constructed	c) eroded
6) striking	a) picketing	b) stunning	c) harsh

FIND-THE-WORDS PUZZLE

You will find words from the article hidden in the box below. Find each word and circle all its letters. To find the words you may have to read from left-to-right, from right-to-left, upward, downward or diagonally. You should be able to find all the words given in the list below the box.

```
Z  L  E  C  T  L  L  A  R  E  V  O
D  A  T  I  N  G  K  V  A  M  U  M
S  N  S  H  A  R  E  S  I  Z  E  A
M  D  I  S  T  A  N  C  E  T  T  R
I  E  H  R  B  F  R  E  N  C  H  I
A  D  Z  N  I  B  C  N  P  N  G  T
L  U  R  E  G  N  A  G  R  I  I  I
C  O  A  T  I  T  S  L  O  T  L  M
B  F  W  V  I  Y  W  I  L  S  F  E
D  O  O  Q  D  L  O  S  E  I  I  F
J  R  N  G  P  R  E  H  A  D  T  Y
P  S  H  D  A  T  L  A  N  T  I  C
```

ATLANTIC	FRENCH
BIG	LANDED
BOND	MARITIME
BORN	NATIONS
CLAIMS	OLD
DATING	OVERALL
DISTANCE	PROVINCE
DISTINCT	ROLE
ENGLISH	SHARE
FLIGHT	SIZE

ANSWER KEY

THE MAIN IDEA

c) The history, size and importance of the four smallest provinces.

UNDERSTANDING WHAT YOU READ

1) The names are: New Brunswick, Nova Scotia, Prince Edward Island and Newfoundland.
2) The distance is nearly 1,300 kilometres. This is about the same as the distance travelled on a flight from Toronto to Halifax.
3) The French were the first to build permanent settlements in the three Maritime provinces. The first was in 1605 in Nova Scotia.
4) Newfoundland is distinct because it lists fishing as its major industry, and many Newfoundlanders share a strong bond with the sea. New Brunswick has its striking landscape of farms and forests and is nicknamed the "Picture Province" for its beautiful scenery. Nova Scotia has Halifax, which is the largest city in Eastern Canada, and Prince Edward Island, Canada's smallest province, is known as the setting for the Anne of Green Gables novels.

REMEMBERING DETAILS

1) T
2) F   The Atlantic Provinces make up less than three percent of the land mass of the entire country.
3) F   The Atlantic Provinces were a battle-zone for many of the earliest North American conflicts between France and Britain.
4) F   Despite their small geography, the Atlantic Provinces play a *big* part in Canada's overall personality.

INFERENCES

1) c
2) b

WORD POWER

1) a
2) b
3) b
4) a
5) a
6) b

FIND-THE-WORDS PUZZLE

	L				L	L	A	R	E	V	O
D	A	T	I	N	G						M
S	N	S	H	A	R	E	S	I	Z	E	A
M	D	I	S	T	A	N	C	E	T	T	R
I	E			B	F	R	E	N	C	H	I
A	D		N	I		C	N		N	G	T
L		R		G	N	A	G	R	I	I	I
C	O			I	T		L	O	T	L	M
B			V	I			I	L	S	F	E
	O	O	O	D	L	O	S	E	I		
	R	N					H		D		
P	S		D	A	T	L	A	N	T	I	C

A

B: Bay of Fundy

1   To describe it, you wouldn't think there was anything unusual about the Bay of Fundy. It is simply a large inlet of the north Atlantic Ocean, which stretches 280 kilometres between the Maritime provinces of New Brunswick and Nova Scotia. It is located along a huge plate of earth called the Continental Shelf in a valley that was once dry land. A rising sea level has since covered the Bay with waters that reach depths of up to 200 metres.

2   It sounds like a typical bay of water you could find anywhere in the world. So what is it that makes the Bay of Fundy such a natural wonder?

3   Try imagining a wave of water reaching nearly 16 metres high, rolling in from the sea with such force it has the power to reverse the flow of an inland river. That's the awesome power behind the Bay of Fundy's famous tides. Starting as a one-metre-high swell on the ocean, the waters of the Bay roll in as part of a massive wave called a tidal bore.

4   At Minas Basin in the upper area of the Bay, these tidal bores can cause water levels to rise and fall 13 metres on average, and as much as 16 metres during spring tides. This gives the Bay of Fundy the highest tides in the entire world. Nearly 100 billion tonnes of water pour into the Bay as the tide peaks, a volume 2,000 times greater than the water flowing out of the St. Lawrence River.

5   The funnel-shape of the Bay of Fundy is the major reason for its giant tides. At its mouth near the Gulf of Maine, the Bay of Fundy is 120 kilometres wide between Yarmouth, Nova Scotia and Cutler, Maine. Further inland beyond Cape D'Or, where the Bay branches off into two channels, the width is reduced to just 45 kilometres at Cape Chignecto. As the Bay narrows, the water levels begin to climb, picking up speed and power as the tides travel inland.

6   Near the head of the Bay, the giant wave is forced upward as it runs out of room to move. It rolls in with such force, streams and rivers that once flowed out towards the sea reverse directions. The huge tides also cover wide areas of mud flats, leaving them submerged until the water begins flowing back out to sea six hours later.

7   At high tide the waters of the Bay of Fundy are home to fin and humpback whales, porpoises and dozens of other sea creatures. When low tide exposes the mud flats, people living along the Bay can hunt for clams, mud-shrimp, mollusks and crabs. The mud flats are also a feeding ground and rest-stop for thousands of migrating birds.

8   Although the Bay of Fundy is known for its natural beauty, there are many people who would like to see the tidal power used to produce electricity. If generating stations were built along the Bay, the rise and fall of Fundy's tides could be a source of power equal to the output of 250 nuclear power plants.

9   This would not only give the Bay of Fundy the highest tides in the world, but also the most powerful!

THE MAIN IDEA

Circle the letter of the sentence which best describes the main idea of the article about the Bay of Fundy. Be prepared to support your answer.

a) The Bay of Fundy hydro-electric project proposal.
b) When to go digging for clams at the bay of Fundy.
c) The Bay of Fundy: A place of incredible tides.
d) Reasons why the Bay of Fundy is simply a large inlet.

UNDERSTANDING WHAT YOU READ

If you can, answer these questions from memory. If you cannot, look back at the article.

1) Where is the Bay of Fundy located?

____

2) What happens when the giant wave reaches the head of the Bay?

____

3) What happens when low tide exposes the mud flats?

____

4) Would the tides at the Bay of Fundy be a good source of electricity?

____

REMEMBERING DETAILS

Write TRUE or FALSE under each statement. If the statement is false, write the statement correctly.

1) The Bay of Fundy's tidal bores, which are massive waves, start as a one-metre-high swell.

____

2) More water flows out of the St. Lawrence River than flows into the Bay of Fundy at high tide.

____

3) The shape of the Bay of Fundy has nothing to do with the tidal bores.

____

4) At high tide there are no sea creatures around the Bay of Fundy.

____

INFERENCES

Based on the article, circle the letter of the best sentence completion.

1) The Bay of Fundy is...

a) quite a tourist attraction.
b) evidence of the power of nature.
c) dangerous for some species of whales.
d) at the centre of a great debate.

2) For many people low tide is...

a) a sign that it is time for them to go catch their dinner.
b) a time when their boat is grounded.
c) a reason to not proceed with a hydroelectric power station.
d) a chance for them to feel safe.

INTERPRETATION

1) Considering what you know about the Bay of Fundy from reading the article, do you think it is appropriate that the power of the tides be used to generate electricity? Discuss.

2) Write a short composition describing how you imagine the Bay of Fundy to be at high and/or low tide.

3) Can you name and describe any other natural wonders of the world?

WORD POWER

Circle the letter of the word that means the same as the word on the left.

1) typical	a) deep	b) picturesque	c) ordinary
2) swell	a) breeze	b) whirlpool	c) wave
3) branches off	a) splits	b) irrigates	c) conquers
4) submerged	a) swirling	b) weighted	c) flooded
5) migrating	a) travelling	b) hibernating	c) tired
6) output	a) transition	b) productivity	c) display

FIND-THE-WORDS PUZZLE

You will find words from the article hidden in the box below. Find each word and circle all its letters. To find the words you may have to read from left-to-right, from right-to-left, upward, downward or diagonally. You should be able to find all the words given in the list below the box.

```
P  D  W  N  A  T  U  R  A  L  C  G
M  O  E  H  R  B  I  N  L  A  N  D
O  B  W  P  A  E  R  O  B  S  P  F
L  E  E  E  T  L  L  Y  C  E  V  N
L  W  T  A  R  H  E  D  H  N  O  M
U  Y  A  A  U  F  S  S  A  N  L  D
S  A  H  V  L  T  U  K  N  O  U  R
K  B  M  T  E  P  Y  L  N  T  M  A
S  C  K  E  S  R  E  V  E  R  E  W
I  N  L  E  T  V  C  K  L  F  E  P
C  R  E  A  T  U  R  E  S  P  G  U
V  A  E  S  T  S  E  H  G  I  H  U
```

BAY	NATURAL
BEAUTY	PLATE
BORE	POWERFUL
CHANNELS	REVERSE
CREATURES	SEA
DEPTHS	TONNES
HIGHEST	UPWARD
INLAND	VOLUME
INLET	WAVE
MOLLUSKS	WHALES

ANSWER KEY

THE MAIN IDEA

c) The Bay of Fundy: A place of incredible tides.

UNDERSTANDING WHAT YOU READ

1) The Bay of Fundy is located between the Maritime provinces of New Brunswick and Nova Scotia. It is located along a huge plate of earth called the Continental Shelf in a valley that was once dry land.
2) When the giant wave reaches the head of the Bay it is forced upward as it runs out of room to move. It rolls in with such force, streams and rivers that once flowed out towards the sea reverse directions. The huge tides also cover wide areas of mud flats, leaving them submerged until the water begins flowing back out to sea six hours later.
3) When low tide exposes the mud flats, people living along the Bay can hunt for clams, mud-shrimp, mollusks and crabs. The mud flats are also a feeding ground and rest-stop for thousands of migrating birds.
4) If generating stations were built along the Bay, the rise and fall of Fundy's tides could be a source of power equal to the output of 250 nuclear power plants.

REMEMBERING DETAILS

1) T
2) F   Nearly 100 billion tonnes of water pour into the Bay as the tide peaks, a volume 2,000 times greater than the water flowing out of the St. Lawrence River.
3) F   The funnel-shape of the Bay of Fundy is the major reason for its giant tides.
4) F   At high tide the waters of the Bay of Fundy are home to fin and humpback whales, porpoises and dozens of other sea creatures.

INFERENCES

1) b
2) a

WORD POWER

1) c
2) c
3) a
4) c
5) a
6) b

FIND-THE-WORDS PUZZLE

```
P   D   W   N   A   T   U   R   A   L
M   O   E   H           I   N   L   A   N   D
O   B   W   P   A   E   R   O   B   S
L   E   E   E   T   L           C   E   V
L   W   T   A   R   H   E           H   N   O
U   Y   A   A   U   F   S   S   A   N   L   D
S   A       V   L   T   U           N   O   U   R
K   B           E   P   Y   L   N   T   M   A
S           E   S   R   E   V   E   R   E   W
I   N   L   E   T                   L           P
C   R   E   A   T   U   R   E   S           U
    A   E   S   T   S   E   H   G   I   H
```

B6

C: CN Tower

1   To get to the top of the world, you have to make a dangerous climb up the highest peak of Mount Everest. But getting to the top of Toronto is as easy as taking a long elevator ride up the side of the CN Tower.

2   Standing high above the city skyline, the CN Tower is not just the tallest building in Toronto. In fact, at slightly over 533 metres, the CN Tower is more than 13 metres higher than Moscow's Ostankino Tower, 100 metres higher than New York's Empire State Building and over 230 metres higher than the Eiffel Tower in Paris. This makes the CN Tower the tallest freestanding tower in the world.

3   The tower is located near Toronto's waterfront on the northern shores of Lake Ontario. Since opening it has become one of the city's most popular tourist attractions. From the indoor "Space Deck" 147 storeys above the ground, tower visitors can enjoy a view of up to 160 kilometres on a clear day. For a more breathtaking look at Toronto, the CN Tower also has an outdoor observation deck featuring the world's highest glass floor. Visitors can literally walk on air 342 metres above the ground! The world's highest and largest revolving restaurant can also be found at the CN Tower.

4   The tower was built over a period of 40 months beginning on February 6, 1973. It was designed to serve as a communications tower used to transmit

television, radio and microwave signals across the country. It cost $57 million to build and was officially opened to the public on June 26, 1976.

5   Before the CN Tower came along, no one had ever built a structure rising so high above the ground. Many experts from around the world were asked to help in planning the design. As a result, a variety of new ideas went into making the tower both the tallest and the safest in the world.

6   For example, the tower was built on a unique Y-shaped foundation dug nearly 15 metres into the ground. This base is concrete over six metres thick, and contains over 500 tons of steel and cable. To protect the tower from fierce winds blowing against its upper half, it was designed to resist winds as strong as 418 kilometres an hour. Even the windows, which are armour-plated, were carefully designed to withstand the constant wind pressure.

7   Four glass elevators provide riders with a birds-eye view as they climb up the outside of the tower to Skypod. This giant donut-shaped structure is nearly seven storeys high and sits over 322 metres above the city near the top of the tower.

8   While nearly 1.7 million visitors are drawn to the tower each year, it has also attracted a number of stunt people. In 1975, a member of the construction crew was the first person to parachute off the tower. In 1986, a man climbed the outside glass windows of the tower twice in one day. Others have run, pogo-sticked, and rode motorcycles up the 2,570 steps to the top.

9   No matter how they get there, visitors to the top agree: there's no better way to see Toronto than from the CN Tower.

THE MAIN IDEA

Circle the letter of the sentence which best describes the main idea of the article about the CN Tower. Be prepared to support your answer.

a) The view from the CN Tower.
b) New ideas put into action.
c) The tower that rivals Mount Everest.
d) The world's tallest freestanding structure.

UNDERSTANDING WHAT YOU READ

If you can, answer these questions from memory. If you cannot, look back at the article.

1) What are some other famous landmarks that the CN Tower is taller than?

____

2) What was the CN tower designed to do?

____

3) What is Skypod?

____

4) What are some of the stunts people have carried out at the CN Tower?

____

REMEMBERING DETAILS

Write TRUE or FALSE under each statement. If the statement is false, write the statement correctly.

1) From "Space Deck" on a clear day you can see at least 5 kilometres into the distance.

____

2) The world's biggest bingo parlour can be found at the CN Tower.

____

3) Three architects from Paris designed the CN Tower.

____

4) There's no better way to see Toronto than from the CN Tower.

____

INFERENCES

Based on the article, circle the letter of the best sentence completion.

1) The CN Tower is so tall that...

a) on a few occasions planes have almost crashed into it.
b) it gets struck by lightening several times a year.
c) it is known all over the world.
d) when the windows break no one volunteers to replace them!

2) The construction of the CN Tower...

a) took longer than it was supposed to.
b) has made daredevils of some people.
c) relied upon engineering and technological breakthroughs.
d) has hurt the cable television industry.

INTERPRETATION

1) Have you ever been to the CN Tower? Or to any other famous, tall structures?
   Which is the tallest building you've ever been in? Discuss.

2) Write a short composition describing what life would be like if the CN Tower
   was your home. How would you decorate it? Who would you live with?
   What special features would your "SkyPad" have?

3) Can you name any other famous Canadian landmarks?

WORD POWER

Circle the letter of the word that means the same as the word on the left.

1) breathtaking	a) closer	b) awesome	c) expensive
2) revolving	a) rotating	b) hesitating	c) elevating
3) transmit	a) black out	b) defect	c) relay
4) constant	a) never-ending	b) howling	c) periodical
5) storeys	a) fables	b) planes	c) floors
6) drawn	a) elevated	b) attracted	c) detracted

FIND-THE-WORDS PUZZLE

You will find words from the article hidden in the box below. Find each word and
circle all its letters. To find the words you may have to read from left-to-right,
from right-to-left, upward, downward or diagonally. You should be able to find all
the words given in the list below the box.

```
S   E   L   E   V   A   T   O   R   F   C   F
A   L   T   O   P   G   W   V   G   X   D   R
F   U   A   K   E   R   A   D   I   O   Y   E
E   V   P   N   U   E   C   L   I   M   B   E
S   L   A   S   G   E   N   I   L   Y   K   S
T   A   O   R   C   I   D   F   W   H   I   T
R   E   W   O   T   E   S   D   O   P   A   A
E   C   E   T   U   H   C   A   R   A   P   N
P   R   P   I   D   E   C   K   L   R   P   D
X   E   E   S   S   A   L   G   D   V   B   I
E   I   A   I   A   R   E   S   I   S   T   N
P   F   K   V   I   E   W   P   T   I   F   G
```

AGREE	RADIO
CLIMB	RESIST
DECK	SAFEST
ELEVATOR	SIGNALS
EXPERTS	SKYLINE
FIERCE	TOP
FREESTANDING	TOWER
GLASS	VIEW
PARACHUTE	VISITORS
PEAK	WORLD

ANSWER KEY

THE MAIN IDEA

d) The world's tallest freestanding structure.

UNDERSTANDING WHAT YOU READ

1) At slightly over 533 metres, the CN Tower is more than 13 metres higher than Moscow's Ostankino Tower, 100 metres higher than New York's Empire State Building and over 230 metres higher than the Eiffel Tower in Paris. This makes the CN Tower the tallest freestanding tower in the world.
2) The CN Tower was designed to serve as a communications tower used to transmit television, radio and microwave signals across the country.
3) Skypod is a giant donut-shaped structure which is nearly seven storeys high and sits over 322 metres above the city near the top of the tower.
4) Stunts people have done at the CN Tower include: parachuting off the tower, climbing the outside glass windows of the tower, running, pogo-sticking and riding a motorcycle up the 2,570 steps to the top.

REMEMBERING DETAILS

1) F From the indoor "Space Deck" 147 storeys above the ground, tower visitors can enjoy a view of up to 160 kilometres on a clear day.
2) F The world's highest and largest revolving restaurant can be found at the CN Tower.
3) F Many experts from around the world were asked to help in planning the design of the CN Tower.
4) T

INFERENCES

1) c
2) c

WORD POWER

1) b
2) a
3) c
4) a
5) c
6) b

FIND-THE-WORDS PUZZLE

```
S  E  L  E  V  A  T  O  R           F
A  L  T  O  P  G                    R
F     A        R  A  D  I     O     E
E        N     E  C  L  I  M     B  E
S        S  G  E  N  I  L     Y  K  S
T        R        I           W        T
R  E  W  O  T        S        O        A
E  C  E  T  U  H  C  A  R     A  P     N
P  R  P  I  D  E  C  K  L              D
X  E  E  S  S  A  L  G  D              I
E  I  A  I     R  E  S  I  S  T        N
   F  K  V  I  E  W                    G
```

D: DEW Line

1   As an active member of the United Nations, Canada has often sent troops on UN peace-keeping missions designed to defend far-away countries from the threat of war. However, there was a time when the threat of an armed attack on North America seemed like a real possibility, and the military was forced to develop plans for the defence of Canada. These plans included the installation of a radar warning system called the Distant Early Warning Line or DEW Line.

2   This line of defence included a chain of ground-based military stations that used radar to provide advance warning of approaching enemy aircraft. Radar is a device that locates an object by bouncing radio waves off of it. The first system was developed in 1935, and it was quickly put to work for military purposes.

3   The DEW Line was built in response to the threat of a nuclear attack on North America launched from the former Soviet Union. This seemed like a real danger during the "Cold War," a period when political differences between the East and West raised fears of atomic war.

4   Following the end of World War II in 1945, Cold War tensions began to develop between Soviet-bloc countries and the Western European allies of the United States. This led both sides into a race to build bigger and better weapons, such as aircraft loaded with

atomic bombs. The most dangerous of these weapons were "ballistic" missiles, long-range bombs capable of being launched at land targets from thousands of miles away.

5   While Canada had air-defence radar systems installed along its Atlantic and Pacific coasts in 1942, they were dismantled after the defeat of Germany and Japan. With the new Soviet threat, the Canadian government began to consider ways to defend the country against a possible attack from the north. The first step was erecting The Pinetree Line, a shared project built by the U.S. and Canada. This system included a network of 33 radar stations running from Vancouver to the Labrador Coast and across the northern U.S. border. In June 1954 the system was upgraded to include the Mid-Canada Line that included 98 more radar stations.

6   Despite the improvements, however, radar experts feared Soviet bombers could still slip through holes in the system. As a result, Canada and the U.S. agreed to build the Distant Early Warning Line across the Canadian Arctic.

7   When it was completed, the DEW Line stretched a total of 8,046 kilometres, including 5,944 kilometres in Canada from Vancouver Island to Baffin Island. It was completed in 1957, and included a total of 22 radar stations that remained in operation protecting Canada for the next 25 years.

8   By the 1980s, weapons-makers had developed low-flying "cruise" missiles. These long-range bombs were designed to avoid radar detection by systems like the DEW and Pinetree lines. As a result, the Canadian government agreed to replace these systems with a modern radar line.

9   Today, it's the North Warning System and not the DEW Line standing on guard in Canada's Far North.

THE MAIN IDEA

Circle the letter of the sentence which best describes the main idea of the article about the DEW Line. Be prepared to support your answer.

a) Canadian peace-keeping missions
b) Canada's use of radar as a line of defence.
c) The invention of radar.
d) The nuclear threat from the former Soviet Union.

UNDERSTANDING WHAT YOU READ

If you can, answer these questions from memory. If you cannot, look back at the article.

1) What is the DEW Line?

____

2) Why was the DEW Line built?

____

3) What was the Pinetree Line?

____

4) When did the DEW Line get replaced? Why?

____

REMEMBERING DETAILS

Write TRUE or FALSE under each statement. If the statement is false, write the statement correctly.

1) Canada is not a member of the United Nations and never sends troops on peace-keeping missions.

____

2) Radar is a device that locates an object by bouncing radio waves off it.

____

3) Ballistic missiles are only capable of being launched at land targets from a short range.

____

4) The DEW Line was completed in 1945 and included 55 radar stations.

____

INFERENCES

Based on the article, circle the letter of the best sentence completion.

1) In spite of the end of the Cold War...

a) the Canadian government still thinks it necessary to maintain a line of defence.
b) Canada and the former Soviet Union have never signed a treaty.
c) ballistic missiles are still being aimed at Canada.
d) Canada and the United States have doubled their line of defence.

2) In the art of building weapons and defence systems...

a) all countries have agreed not to design any new nuclear weapons.
b) Canada is a world leader.
c) the North Warning System will never be bettered.
d) trying to stay ahead of the designs of other military powers is an ongoing struggle.

INTERPRETATION

1) Is world peace only a dream or is it a real possibility? What are some things
   that can be done to achieve world peace? Discuss.

2) In recent times there has been much discussion as to whether Canadian troops
   should continue to be sent on peace-keeping missions, to try to prevent warring
   factions from killing each other. Should these missions continue? What is
   your opinion? Discuss.

3) You have been asked to give a speech at the United Nations on why world
   peace must be achieved now. As a class you can brainstorm some ideas for
   your speeches. Then write the speeches and deliver them to your classmates.

WORD POWER

Circle the letter of the word that means the same as the word on the left.

1) installation   a) establishment   b) restoration   c) implication

2) launched   a) progressed   b) threatened   c) fired

3) dismantled   a) remodeled   b) torn down   c) improved

4) project   a) undertaking   b) gamble   c) missile

5) upgraded   a) requested   b) tested   c) improved

6) avoid   a) attack   b) divert   c) duck

FIND-THE-WORDS PUZZLE

You will find words from the article hidden in the box below. Find each word and circle all its letters. To find the words you may have to read from left-to-right, from right-to-left, upward, downward or diagonally. You should be able to find all the words given in the list below the box.

```
V  R  W  T  Y  D  E  H  O  L  E  S
M  A  A  E  B  O  M  B  E  R  S  A
I  D  V  N  E  L  B  A  P  A  C  I
S  A  E  S  O  G  I  O  I  D  A  R
S  R  S  I  T  A  E  F  E  D  P  C
I  T  R  O  O  P  S  V  V  C  R  R
L  G  A  N  D  O  I  L  P  U  F  A
E  I  S  S  V  C  F  N  I  E  M  F
S  B  N  I  E  D  I  S  T  A  N  T
W  P  E  E  Y  C  E  R  D  R  O  O
S  T  A  T  I  O  N  S  S  L  I  P
G  N  I  N  R  A  W  A  G  Y  E  S
```

AIRCRAFT	MISSILES
BOMBERS	RADAR
CAPABLE	RADIO
CRUISE	SLIP
DEFEAT	SOVIET
DEVICE	STATIONS
DISTANT	TENSIONS
EARLY	TROOPS
HOLES	WARNING
LINE	WAVES

ANSWER KEY

THE MAIN IDEA

b) Canada's use of radar as a line of defence.

UNDERSTANDING WHAT YOU READ

1) The Dew Line is the Distant Early Warning Line. It is a line of defence which included a chain of ground-based military stations that used radar to provide advance warning of approaching enemy aircraft.
2) The DEW Line was built in response to the threat of a nuclear attack on North America launched from the former Soviet Union.
3) The Pinetree Line, a shared project built by the U.S. and Canada, was a defence system which included a network of 33 radar stations running from Vancouver to the Labrador Coast and across the northern U.S. border.
4) By the 1980s, the Canadian government agreed to replace the DEW Line with a more modern radar line. By this time weapons-makers had developed low-flying "cruise" missiles. These long-range bombs were designed to avoid radar detection by systems like the DEW and Pinetree lines.

REMEMBERING DETAILS

1) F   Canada is an active member of the United Nations and has often sent troops on UN peace-keeping missions designed to defend far-away countries from the threat of war.
2) T
3) F   Ballistic missiles are long-range bombs capable of being launched at land targets from thousands of miles away.
4) F   The DEW Line was completed in 1957 and included a total of 22 radar stations that remained in operation protecting Canada for the next 25 years.

INFERENCES

1) a
2) d

WORD POWER

1) a
2) c
3) b
4) a
5) c
6) c

FIND-THE-WORDS PUZZLE

```
       R   W   T                   H   O   L   E   S
 M  A  A   E   B   O   M   B   E   R   S   A
 I  D  V   N   E   L   B   A   P   A   C   I
 S  A  E   S                   O   I   D   A   R
 S  R  S   I   T   A   E   F   E   D           C
 I  T  R   O   O   P   S   V                   R   R
 L        N           O   I               U        A
 E  I     S   V   C               I   E        F
 S     N  I   E   D   I   S   T   A   N   T
       E  E                       E           R
 S  T  A  T   I   O   N   S   S   L   I   P
 G  N  I  N   R   A   W                   Y
```

E: Ellesmere Island National Park

1   Mother Nature may be responsible for creating much of Canada's natural scenic beauty. But it is Canada's national park system that has helped to preserve it for everyone to enjoy.

2   As one of the largest government agencies of its kind in the world, Canada's parks department oversees 34 national parks and park reserves, and over 600 provincial parks. Within park boundaries can be found the most spectacular scenery the Canadian wilderness has to offer, from raging rivers to frozen icefields, and from blankets of thick forest to barren, rocky plains.

3   Located as far south as the border of Northern California, and north beyond the Arctic Circle, Canada's many parks attract over 13 million visitors each year. Only about 400 of these visitors, however, manage to make the long trip north to Ellesmere Island National Park Reserve in the Northwest Territories.

4   The reserve has the most isolated location of all of Canada's national parks, sitting on the northern tip of Ellesmere Island. This 122,000 square kilometre chunk of frozen wilderness is the northernmost island in North America. It is located just 800 kilometres from the North Pole, a four-hour flight from one of the most remote communities in Canada, Resolute Bay on Cornwallis Island.

5   Ellesmere Island is known for long harsh winters, short cool summers,

cold dry winds and very little rain or snow. In fact, Ellesmere is considered a polar desert, since less than 6 centimetres of rain and snow fall on the island each year.

6   Because of current aboriginal land claims, Ellesmere Island Park is still considered a reserve. It opened in 1986, when 39,500 square kilometres were set aside through the National Parks Act to preserve the area. After Wood Buffalo National Park, it is the second largest "preserve" in Canada.

7   Fossils of snakes, lizards and even alligators found on the island indicate that, hundreds of thousands of years ago, it was once a swamp. But drastic changes in the weather have left Ellesmere covered in snow glaciers, some up to 40 kilometres long. Icefields as much as 900 metres thick cover much of the island, as well as the Grantland Mountains in the northern section of the park. Mount Barbeau, an icy peak 2,604 metres high, is the highest mountain in eastern North America.

While Ellesmere Island National 8 Park Reserve may sound like a barren wasteland, it actually supports a variety of plant and animal life. Most of this is found near Lake Hagen, the largest lake north of the Arctic circle. The area around this eighty-kilometre-long lake is rich with wildlife, including Peary caribou, arctic wolves, fox and hares, polar bears and musk ox. For a few weeks each summer, lush meadows and arctic wildflowers bring colour to land normally covered with white.

Though few people visit Ellesmere 9 National Park Reserve, it remains one of Canada's most beautiful national parks.

THE MAIN IDEA

Circle the letter of the sentence which best describes the main idea of the article about Ellesmere Island National Park Reserve. Be prepared to support your answer.

a) The story of a worthless wasteland.
b) Canada's most isolated National Park.
c) The brave people who visit Ellesmere Island.
d) Wildlife in Canada's north.

UNDERSTANDING WHAT YOU READ

If you can, answer these questions from memory. If you cannot, look back at the article.

1) What can be found within the boundaries of Canada's parks?

2) Where is Ellesmere Island National Park Reserve located?

3) What effect has drastic changes in the weather had on Ellesmere Island?

4) What kinds of wildlife can be found in the Ellesmere Island National Park Reserve?

REMEMBERING DETAILS

Write TRUE or FALSE under each statement. If the statement is false, write the statement correctly.

1) Ellesmere Island National Park Reserve is in a highly populated neighbourhood just outside of Calgary.

2) Ellesmere Island is known for long hot summers and short mild winters.

3) Even in the summertime nothing grows on Ellesmere Island.

4) Few people visit Ellesmere Island National Park Reserve.

INFERENCES

Based on the article, circle the letter of the best sentence completion.

1) In the past...

a) the weather was much warmer on Ellesmere Island.
b) many people used to visit Ellesmere Island.
c) Ellesmere Island National Park Reserve was much smaller.
d) you could only get to Ellesmere Island by dog sleigh.

2) Not many people visit Ellesmere Island National Park Reserve because...

a) polar bears have been known to attack the tourists.
b) it is in such a remote and isolated place.
c) people are afraid of frostbite.
d) it is not open to the public.

INTERPRETATION

1) Make a list of ten things you would need to have with you to survive on
   Ellesmere Island.

2) Somehow you have been left alone on Ellesmere Island. Fortunately, you have
   your ten items from question number one. Write a short composition
   describing how you got there, and how you survived while you were there.
   You can end your story by describing how you got off the island.

3) Can you name any other National or Provincial Parks in Canada? Have you
   been to any? Describe your visit there. In pairs, go to the library and find
   information about another park in Canada. Report back to the class.

WORD POWER

Circle the letter of the word that means the same as the word on the left.

1) boundaries	a) limits	b) restrictions	c) yards
2) raging	a) turbulent	b) calm	c) deep
3) isolated	a) inhabited	b) wilderness	c) removed
4) current	a) old	b) ongoing	c) settled
5) drastic	a) capital	b) extreme	c) slender
6) lush	a) barren	b) overgrown	c) rich

FIND-THE-WORDS PUZZLE

You will find words from the article hidden in the box below. Find each word and circle all its letters. To find the words you may have to read from left-to-right, from right-to-left, upward, downward or diagonally. You should be able to find all the words given in the list below the box.

S	R	E	I	C	A	L	G	Y	C	I	A
G	E	S	L	D	R	H	P	M	E	V	G
X	M	C	M	I	C	F	A	L	I	F	E
P	O	L	A	R	T	O	P	R	W	K	N
R	T	H	N	R	I	S	A	M	S	E	C
E	E	D	A	M	C	S	N	V	A	H	I
S	S	N	G	X	W	I	E	B	U	W	E
E	G	A	E	O	F	L	R	S	T	N	S
R	B	L	D	K	X	S	R	P	A	R	K
V	W	A	S	T	E	L	A	N	D	L	Y
E	E	P	Y	F	Y	D	B	N	I	A	R
M	S	E	E	S	R	E	V	O	F	O	X

AGENCIES	MANAGE
ARCTIC	MEADOWS
BARREN	OVERSEES
FOSSILS	PARK
FOX	POLAR
GLACIERS	PRESERVE
HARSH	RAIN
ICY	REMOTE
LAND	SWAMP
LIFE	WASTELAND

ANSWER KEY

THE MAIN IDEA

b) Canada's most isolated National Park.

UNDERSTANDING WHAT YOU READ

1) Within park boundaries can be found the most spectacular scenery the Canadian wilderness has to offer, from raging rivers to frozen icefields, and from blankets of thick forest to barren, rocky plains.
2) Ellesmere Island National Park Reserve sits on the northern tip of Ellesmere Island in the Northwest Territories. This 122,000 square kilometre chunk of frozen wilderness is the northernmost island in North America. It is located just 800 kilometres from the North Pole.
3) Drastic changes in the weather have left Ellesmere Island covered in snow glaciers, some up to 40 kilometres long.
4) Ellesmere Island National Park Reserve is rich with wildlife, including Peary caribou, arctic wolves, fox and hares, polar bears and musk ox.

REMEMBERING DETAILS

1) F   The reserve has the most isolated location of all of Canada's national parks, sitting on the northern tip of Ellesmere Island.
2) F   Ellesmere Island is known for long harsh winters and short cool summers.
3) F   For a few weeks each summer, lush meadows and Arctic wildflowers bring colour to Ellesmere Island.
4) T

INFERENCES

1) a
2) b

WORD POWER

1) a
2) a
3) c
4) b
5) b
6) c

FIND-THE-WORDS PUZZLE

S	R	E	I	C	A	L	G	Y	C	I	A
	E				R	H					G
	M		M		C	F	A	L	I	F	E
P	O	L	A	R	T	O	P	R			N
R	T		N		I	S		M	S		C
E	E	D	A		C	S	N		A	H	I
S		N	G		W	I	E			W	E
E		A	E	O		L	R				S
R		L	D			S	R	P	A	R	K
V	W	A	S	T	E	L	A	N	D		
E	E						B	N	I	A	R
M	S	E	E	S	R	E	V	O	F	O	X

F: Forty-Ninth Parallel

1   In geographic terms, a parallel of latitude is an invisible line drawn around the earth used to measure distances north and south of the earth's mid-point (called the equator). By following these lines north from the equator to the 49th parallel of latitude, you'll discover the borderline that separates the world's two friendliest neighbours, Canada and the United States.

2   The official border shared by Canada and the United States measures a total length of 6,418.1 kilometres. This long frontier runs from the Atlantic Ocean to the Pacific Ocean, and also includes the northern boundary between the American state of Alaska and Canada's Yukon Territory.

3   More than 40 percent of the border between the two countries runs through shared waterways, mostly in the Great Lakes/St. Lawrence River region. However, an equally large distance runs westward from Ontario along the 49th parallel. From the Lake of the Woods region to the Pacific Coast, the border along the 49th parallel is the world's longest international border running in a continuous line.

4   Even more amazing is the fact the Canada/U.S. border remains almost unguarded by either country. That tradition dates back as far as 1870, when officials representing both governments signed the Treaty of Washington. The treaty reduced the

risk of an armed clash along the border and paved the way for closer ties between Canada and the United States.

5   This agreement followed many years of armed conflict between the two young countries, both of which were fighting for survival on the North American continent. Before Canada entered into Confederation in 1867, six different armies from the south had invaded Canadian territory. This included an American attack on Quebec as early as December 6, 1775. In return, armies based on Canadian soil, supported by British troops, had been responsible for the invasion and destruction of several American cities over the years.

6   The low point in relations between the two countries came on June 18, 1812, when war was declared between the U.S. and Canada. With less than 10,000 troops, Canada looked to be no match for the 175,000 men available to fight for the American side. In fact, Thomas Jefferson, then President of the United States, declared that the conquest of Canada was "a mere matter of marching."

7   However, British victories over American armies at Detroit and Fort Niagara proved the President was wrong, and the war dragged on. When the the Treaty of Ghent finally brought the war to an end in December 1814, it marked the last time the two countries would ever oppose each other in battle.

8   Today the Canada/U.S. border is one of the busiest in the world, as millions of people from both countries move freely across the 49th parallel. Bridges, tunnels, roads and railways are just a few of the cross-border travel routes that link the two countries.

9   On a map, the 49th parallel appears to be a line that separates Canada from the United States. However, people on both sides of the border now see it more as a symbol of the peaceful relationship that brings these two great nations together.

THE MAIN IDEA

Circle the letter of the sentence which best describes the main idea of the article about the Forty-Ninth Parallel. Be prepared to support your answer.

a) The world's friendliest neighbours.
b) Wars between Canada and the United States.
c) Why Canada and the United States get along so well.
d) The world's longest undefended border.

UNDERSTANDING WHAT YOU READ

If you can, answer these questions from memory. If you cannot, look back at the article.

1) What is a parallel of latitude?

2) When was the Treaty of Washington signed. What did it do?

3) What was the low point in relations between the United States and Canada?

4) Name some cross-border travel routes that link Canada and the United States.

REMEMBERING DETAILS

Write TRUE or FALSE under each statement. If the statement is false, write the statement correctly.

1) The official border shared by Canada and the United States measures a total length of 6,418.1 kilometres.

2) The Canada/United States border is one of the most heavily guarded in the world.

3) No armies from south of the border have ever invaded Canada.

4) The last time Canada and the United States waged war against each other was in 1963.

INFERENCES

Based on the article, circle the letter of the best sentence completion.

1) The fact that the border between Canada and the United States is unguarded...

a) is a sign that both countries have weak governments.
b) proves that relations between the two countries are very good.
c) shows that neither country cares about contraband crossing its borders.
d) could cause trouble in the future.

2) The fact that the greatly outnumbered troops defending Canada could not be
   beaten...

a) proves that Canadians are more patriotic than Americans.
b) illustrates that a greater number of soldiers does not always guarantee victory.
c) shows that the Americans were lousy shots.
d) could be because the Americans could not stand the cold weather in Canada.

INTERPRETATION

1) Many people believe that Canada will eventually become part of the United
   States. List reasons why this would be a good idea, and reasons why it would
   not be a good idea.

2) Using an atlas or a globe, check and write down on which parallel of latitude
   some major Canadian cities lie. Follow these lines of latitude around the
   world. List other important foreign cities which lie on the same or
   approximately the same lines.

3) Do you think Canada and the United States will ever go to war against each
   other in the future? What could cause such a conflict to begin? What would
   be the result? Discuss.

WORD POWER

Circle the letter of the word that means the same as the word on the left.

1) continuous	a) jagged	b) rugged	c) uninterrupted
2) tradition	a) practice	b) extradition	c) symbol
3) soil	a) bases	b) land	c) methods
4) able	a) optimistic	b) allied	c) skilled
5) mere	a) precise	b) simple	c) plotted
6) dragged on	a) escalated	b) continued	c) ceased

FIND-THE-WORDS PUZZLE

You will find words from the article hidden in the box below. Find each word and circle all its letters. To find the words you may have to read from left-to-right, from right-to-left, upward, downward or diagonally. You should be able to find all the words given in the list below the box.

```
E  Q  U  A  T  O  R  N  O  K  U  Y
K  N  T  Y  T  A  E  R  T  S  K  T
R  P  I  N  V  A  S  I  O  N  U  E
C  L  L  L  T  Y  G  B  Y  O  M  P
O  E  A  I  R  I  R  E  G  I  O  N
N  L  T  C  O  E  E  A  C  T  S  D
T  L  I  T  Q  S  D  S  V  A  T  A
I  A  T  Y  L  E  E  R  F  N  L  K
N  R  U  U  S  Y  M  B  O  L  Y  S
E  A  D  V  P  Q  H  T  O  B  L  A
N  P  E  A  C  E  F  U  L  G  S  L
T  B  M  R  E  I  T  N  O  R  F  A
```

ALASKA	MOSTLY
BORDERLINE	NATIONS
BOTH	PARALLEL
CONTINENT	PEACEFUL
EQUATOR	REGION
FREELY	SOIL
FRONTIER	SYMBOL
INVASION	TIES
LATITUDE	TREATY
MAP	YUKON

ANSWER KEY

THE MAIN IDEA

d) The world's longest undefended border.

UNDERSTANDING WHAT YOU READ

1) A parallel of latitude is an invisible line drawn around the earth used to measure distances north and south of the earth's mid-point, which is called the equator.
2) In 1870 officials representing both governments signed the Treaty of Washington. The treaty reduced the risk of an armed clash along the border and paved the way for closer ties between Canada and the United States.
3) The low point in relations between the two countries came on June 18, 1812, when war was declared between the U.S. and Canada.
4) Bridges, tunnels, roads and railways are just a few of the cross-border travel routes that link the two countries.

REMEMBERING DETAILS

1) T
2) F   The Canada/U.S. border remains almost unguarded by either country.
3) F   Before Canada had entered into Confederation in 1867, six different armies from the south had invaded Canadian territory.
4) F   December 1814 was the last time Canada and the United States opposed each other in battle.

INFERENCES

1) b
2) b

WORD POWER

1) c
2) a
3) b
4) c
5) b
6) b

FIND-THE-WORDS PUZZLE

E	Q	U	A	T	O	R	N	O	K	U	Y
	N		Y	T	A	E	R	T	S		
		I	N	V	A	S	I	O	N		
C	L	L	L	T					O	M	
O	E	A	I	R	I	R	E	G	I	O	N
N	L	T		O	E	E			T	S	
T	L	I			S	D	S		A	T	A
I	A	T	Y	L	E	E	R	F	N	L	K
N	R	U		S	Y	M	B	O	L	Y	S
E	A	D		P		H	T	O	B		A
N	P	E	A	C	E	F	U	L			L
T		M	R	E	I	T	N	O	R	F	A

G: The Great Lakes

1   They have been called "a river of inland seas," five giant bodies of water that cover 244,650 square kilometres. From Duluth, Minnesota in the west to the St. Lawrence River in the east, the Great Lakes stretch over 3,000 kilometres. When measured together, Lakes Superior, Huron, Michigan, Erie and Ontario make up by far the largest body of fresh water in the world.

2   The Great Lakes create a natural barrier between the central United States and Canada. The international border between the countries passes through the middle of all the lakes except Lake Michigan, which lies completely in the U.S.

3   Lake Superior, the largest of the Great Lakes, is located farthest to the west. It is also the deepest of all the Great Lakes, reaching down 405 metres at its lowest point (by comparison, Lake Erie measures only 64 metres at its deepest point). Lake Ontario, the smallest in terms of surface area, lies farthest to the east. Here the lakes drain out to the sea through the St. Lawrence River.

4   Although they are among the world's largest, the Great Lakes are considered five of the youngest. Their present shapes and sizes were formed only 10,000 years ago. The lake-beds were carved into the earth during the last Ice Age, when huge mountains of ice called glaciers moved back and forth over the land.

5   As the glaciers began moving north nearly 15,000 years ago, much of the remaining ice began melting. This helped create huge super-sized lakes that covered much of what is now Canada. As the water drained into the sea, the levels of these giant lakes began to drop. Thousands of smaller lakes were eventually formed, including the five Great Lakes.

6   The earliest settlers in the Great Lakes region were North American Indian tribes. Among the large tribes living in the area were the Ojibway, Ottawa, Neutral, and Iroquois Indians. They relied on the waterways for fishing, fur trapping and travelling. Two of the lakes, Huron and Erie, were named after the Indian tribes that lived along their shores, while the names of Lake Ontario and Lake Michigan were taken from Indian words.

7   French fur traders were probably the first Europeans to travel across the Great Lakes. Famous explorers like Champlain and LaSalle helped open up the waterways to a rush of French and British settlers into the area. They looked at the region's vast fur trade as a new source of wealth for their homelands. Soon France and Britain were fighting for possession of the entire Great Lakes region in a war eventually won by the British.

8   The fight for control of the Great Lakes continued right through the War of 1812 between that U.S. and Canada. However, when the war finally ended, settlement in and around the lakes was rapid on both sides of the border.

9   Today the Great Lakes region balances beautiful scenery with some of North America's largest cities. This is one reason why these "great" lakes continue to live up to their name.

THE MAIN IDEA

Circle the letter of the sentence which best describes the main idea of the article about the Great Lakes. Be prepared to support your answer.

a) The largest body of fresh water in the world.
b) Battles for the Great Lakes.
c) The Indian tribes who lived near the Great Lakes.
d) The Great Lakes fur trade.

UNDERSTANDING WHAT YOU READ

If you can, answer these questions from memory. If you cannot, look back at the article.

1) What are the names of the five Great Lakes?

---

2) When and how were the present shapes and sizes of the Great Lakes formed?

---

3) What did explorers like Champlain and LaSalle help to do?

---

4) Why were the early explorers so interested in the Great Lakes region?

REMEMBERING DETAILS

Write TRUE or FALSE under each statement. If the statement is false, write the statement correctly.

1) From Lake Erie the Great Lakes drain out to sea through the Mississippi River.

---

2) The Great Lakes have been around for millions of years.

---

3) The earliest settlers in the Great Lakes region were North American Indian tribes.

---

4) France and Britain never argued about the Great Lakes.

INFERENCES

Based on the article, circle the letter of the best sentence completion.

1) They are called the Great Lakes because...

a) there is no salt in the water.
b) so many people depend upon them for their livelihood.
c) they are so big.
d) they formed when "great" glaciers melted.

2) Champlain and LaSalle opened up the Great Lakes region to exploration by...

a) reporting back to their countrymen of the great wealth of furs in the area.
b) making friends with the Indians in the area.
c) finding a route to help bypass Niagara Falls.
d) waging war against British settlers in the area.

INTERPRETATION

1) Do you think another Ice Age is possible? Why? Why not? What would
    happen if one did occur? Discuss.

2) Many cities were founded near water. Look at a map of North America. List
   twenty-five major North American cities and the bodies of water near which
   each is located.

3) Millions of people rely on the Great Lakes for their drinking water and for
   other things. Write a short composition describing what would happen if the
   Great Lakes dried up.

WORD POWER

Circle the letter of the word that means the same as the word on the left.

1) barrier	a) wall	b) bridge	c) playground
2) lies	a) trains	b) airs	c) rests
3) drain	a) overload	b) empty	c) melt
4) relied on	a) caught on	b) counted on	c) came upon
5) rapid	a) quick	b) escalating	c) energetic
6) live up to	a) meet up with	b) expand	c) deserve

FIND-THE-WORDS PUZZLE

You will find words from the article hidden in the box below. Find each word and circle all its letters. To find the words you may have to read from left-to-right, from right-to-left, upward, downward or diagonally. You should be able to find all the words given in the list below the box.

R	F	I	S	H	I	N	G	V	P	E	O
A	E	I	W	U	L	R	L	U	M	N	H
W	I	G	V	F	P	D	A	A	T	W	U
T	R	I	B	E	S	E	R	A	K	F	R
M	E	L	T	I	N	G	R	O	W	E	C
I	F	I	G	H	T	I	V	I	P	B	S
C	O	W	D	F	O	E	X	Y	O	O	X
H	P	X	E	X	P	L	O	R	E	R	S
I	D	B	M	T	S	E	P	E	E	D	R
G	N	O	R	U	H	L	A	D	T	E	U
A	V	H	O	H	T	L	A	E	W	R	F
N	A	A	F	C	A	R	V	E	D	S	C

BORDER	FUR
CARVED	HURON
DEEPEST	LAKES
DROP	MELTING
ERIE	MICHIGAN
EXPLORERS	ONTARIO
FIGHT	SUPERIOR
FIVE	TRIBES
FORMED	WAR
FISHING	WEALTH

ANSWER KEY

THE MAIN IDEA

a) The largest body of fresh water in the world.

UNDERSTANDING WHAT YOU READ

1) The names of the Great Lakes are Lake Superior, Lake Huron, Lake Michigan, Lake Erie and Lake Ontario.
2) Their present shapes and sizes were formed only 10,000 years ago. The lake-beds were carved into the earth during the last Ice Age, when huge mountains of ice called glaciers moved back and forth over the land.
3) Champlain and LaSalle helped open up the waterways to a rush of French and British settlers into the area.
4) The early explorers looked at the region's vast fur trade as a new source of wealth for their homelands.

REMEMBERING DETAILS

1) F   The Great Lakes drain from Lake Ontario out to the sea through the St. Lawrence River.
2) F   The Great Lakes are considered five of the youngest lakes in the world and have only been around in their present shapes and sizes for only about 10,000 years.
3) T
4) F   France and Britain fought for possession of the entire Great Lakes region in a war eventually won by the British.

INFERENCES

1) c
2) a

WORD POWER

1) a
2) c
3) b
4) b
5) a
6) c

FIND-THE-WORDS PUZZLE

```
R  F  I     S  H  I  N  G              O
A  E  I        U           L        N
W  I     V        P  D        A  T
T  R  I  B  E  S  E  R  A  K
M  E  L  T  I  N  G  R  O        E
I  F  I  G  H  T  I        I  P  B  S
C           D     O              O  O
H           E  X  P  L  O  R  E  R  S
I           M  T  S  E  P  E  E  D  R
G  N  O  R  U  H              E  U
A           O  H  T  L  A  E  W  R  F
N           F  C  A  R  V  E  D
```

H: Head-Smashed-In Buffalo Jump

1   A little over 150 years ago, a brave young member of the Blackfoot Indian tribe waited eagerly at the bottom of a 10 metre high cliff. Up above, on the dusty plain leading toward the cliff, other tribe members were busy trying to lead a stampeding herd of wild buffalo to jump over the edge. As the young Indian watched, hundreds of buffalo came crashing over the cliff, falling to their death and piling up at the bottom of the ledge.

2   When the hunters climbed down to butcher the buffalo, they discovered their friend had been killed, the result of a crushed skull. To honour him, they gave the site the Blackfoot name Estipah-Skikni-kots, meaning "where he got his head smashed in."

3   So goes the story of how Canada's most famous "buffalo jump" got its name. Long before Europeans arrived with their guns, Indians of the Canadian plains often relied on buffalo jumps when hunting. A successful buffalo hunt helped supply the Indians with meat for food, bones for weapons and tools, and hides for clothing and shelter. Luring a large herd of buffalo over the cliffs was a fast and effective way to re-supply Indian tribes and their families with important materials.

4   Head-Smashed-In Buffalo Jump is located just 17 kilometres northwest of where Fort MacLeod, Alberta is now located. Evidence uncovered at the site suggests it may have been used by different tribes for as long as 5,500

years. This makes it one of the oldest buffalo jumps in North America. Besides being considered a sacred place by Canada's Native people, Head-Smashed-In Buffalo Jump has been declared a World Heritage Site. This is a similar honour given to such other famous historical locations as the Pyramids and Stonehenge.

5   Although using a buffalo jump sounds like an easy way to hunt, luring the herd over the cliff was a very difficult task. Such hunts could involve hundreds of warriors, who often had to follow a herd for days. Many of the hunters dressed in wolf and buffalo skins and ran alongside the herd. Their job was to confuse the female leaders of the herd and cause them to stampede. As they approached the cliff at speeds of close to 50 kilometres an hour, it was impossible to turn around, and the buffalo plunged to their death.

6   At one time over 60 million buffalo roamed the regions of the North American plains, which provided Indian hunters with a steady source of food. However, the arrival of Europeans and their guns put an end to the great buffalo herds. While buffalo were once solely hunted for survival, they were soon being hunted for sport. By the mid-1800s, the herds were nearly wiped out.

7   In July 1987, England's Duke and Duchess of York were on hand at Head-Smashed-In Buffalo Jump to officially open a $10 million museum and tourist centre at the site. And though it may be remembered as a place where thousands of buffalo met a cruel death, Head-Smashed-In Buffalo Jump is also a place that helped ensure the survival of Native People on the plains for thousands of years.

THE MAIN IDEA

Circle the letter of the sentence which best describes the main idea of the article about Head-Smashed-In Buffalo Jump. Be prepared to support your answer.

a) World Heritage Sites.
b) Why buffalo nearly became extinct.
c) Secret Indian hunting techniques.
d) The story of a sacred hunting ground.

UNDERSTANDING WHAT YOU READ

If you can, answer these questions from memory. If you cannot, look back at the article.

1) How did Head-Smashed-In Buffalo Jump get its name?

____

2) Why did the Native people hunt buffalo?

____

3) Why did buffalo nearly become wiped out?

____

4) Who was on hand when the Head-Smashed-In Buffalo Jump Museum was opened?

____

REMEMBERING DETAILS

Write TRUE or FALSE under each statement. If the statement is false, write the statement correctly.

1) Indians of the Canadian plains killed buffalo for sport.

____

2) Evidence uncovered at the site suggests this buffalo jump may have been used by different tribes for as long as 5,500 years.

____

3) Using a buffalo jump was a very easy way to hunt buffalo.

____

4) Head-Smashed-In Buffalo Jump had nothing to do with the survival of the Native people on the plains.

____

INFERENCES

Based on the article, circle the letter of the best sentence completion.

1) Head-Smashed-In Buffalo Jump...

a) is visited by millions of tourists every year.
b) was also used for hunting caribou.
c) is recognized as an important site in the history of mankind.
d) is the second oldest buffalo jump in North America.

2) Native people...

a) respected the buffalo and only killed as many as they needed to survive.
b) would have killed more buffalo if they had had guns.
c) were opposed to the opening of the museum.
d) relied more on fishing than hunting.

INTERPRETATION

1) Write a short composition describing a buffalo hunt at Head-Smashed-In
   Buffalo Jump. You can choose from whose point of view you want to view the
   hunt. Choices can include: from a buffalo's point of view or from a Native
   person's point of view.

2) Whenever people think of Head-Smashed-In Buffalo Jump they probably think
   of the Native warrior who lost his life there. In a way this place is named after
   him. Would you be willing to lose your life, but in such a way that you would
   be remembered forever? How would you lose your life? Discuss.

3) Research another World Heritage Site and make a short presentation describing
   it to the rest of the class.

WORD POWER

Circle the letter of the word that means the same as the word on the left.

1) eagerly	a) passionately	b) anxiously	c) severely
2) luring	a) scaring	b) managing	c) enticing
3) uncovered	a) unaffected	b) placed	c) found
4) solely	a) only	b) obviously	c) viciously
5) wiped out	a) rejuvenated	b) obliterated	c) caught on
6) cruel	a) quick	b) brutal	c) terminal

FIND-THE-WORDS PUZZLE

You will find words from the article hidden in the box below. Find each word and circle all its letters. To find the words you may have to read from left-to-right, from right-to-left, upward, downward or diagonally. You should be able to find all the words given in the list below the box.

S	I	R	O	A	M	I	N	G	O	R	S
L	J	C	L	J	U	M	P	Y	R	H	A
O	A	L	A	U	S	N	T	A	E	M	C
O	P	O	F	G	E	G	D	C	K	E	R
T	D	T	F	Y	U	S	N	U	G	G	E
H	S	H	U	K	M	E	E	H	S	A	D
U	N	I	B	E	D	E	P	M	A	T	S
N	O	N	J	I	Y	T	A	E	G	I	Y
T	P	G	V	D	E	T	I	S	H	R	E
E	A	E	A	R	R	I	V	A	L	E	A
R	E	S	C	F	R	E	T	L	E	H	S
S	W	M	K	O	L	U	H	J	U	M	K

ARRIVAL	MEAT
BUFFALO	MUSEUM
CLOTHING	ROAMING
DUSTY	SACRED
EVIDENCE	SHELTER
GUNS	SITE
HERD	STAMPEDE
HERITAGE	TASK
HUNTERS	TOOLS
JUMP	WEAPONS

H5

ANSWER KEY

THE MAIN IDEA

d) The story of a sacred hunting ground.

UNDERSTANDING WHAT YOU READ

1) It got its name to honour an Indian who was at the bottom of the cliff when the buffalo came stampeding over the edge. The Indian's skull was crushed. Thus the name: Head-Smashed-In Buffalo Jump.
2) The Native people hunted buffalo to supply themselves with meat for food, bones for weapons and tools, and hides for clothing and shelter.
3) The arrival of Europeans and their guns put an end to the great buffalo herds. While buffalo were once solely hunted for survival, they were soon being hunted for sport. By the mid-1800s, the herds were nearly wiped out.
4) England's Duke and Duchess of York were on hand at the opening of the Head-Smashed-In Buffalo Jump Museum.

REMEMBERING DETAILS

1) F   Indians of the Canadian plains killed buffalo for meat for food, for bones for weapons and for tools, and for hides for clothing and for shelter.
2) T
3) F   Although a buffalo jump sounds like an easy way to hunt, luring the herd over the cliff was a very difficult task. Such hunts could involve hundreds of warriors, who often had to follow a herd for days.
4) F   Head-Smashed-In Buffalo Jump is a place that helped ensure the survival of Native people on the plains for thousands of years.

INFERENCES

1) c
2) a

WORD POWER

1) b
2) c
3) c
4) a
5) b
6) b

FIND-THE-WORDS PUZZLE

```
S     R  O  A  M  I  N  G           S
L     C  L  J  U  M  P              A
O     L  A     S     T  A  E  M     C
O     O  F     E     D  C        E  R
T     T  F     U  S  N  U  G  G     E
H  S  H  U     M  E           S  A  D
U  N  I  B  E  D  E  P  M  A  T     S
N  O  N        I                 I  Y
T  P  G  V  D  E  T  I  S        R
E  A  E  A  R  R  I  V  A  L  E
R  E  S     R  E  T  L  E  H     S
S  W     K           H
```

I: Icefields Parkway

1   To someone reading a road map, the Icefields Parkway appears to be nothing more than a tiny ribbon of highway heading northwest through the rugged Canadian Rocky Mountains. But anyone travelling along it knows that the Icefields Parkway is more than just another highway. In fact, it is one of the most spectacular scenic routes in all of Canada.

2   Winding its way along a 230 kilometre stretch from Lake Louise to Jasper, the Parkway crosses through the boundaries of both Banff and Jasper National Parks in Alberta. This route offers travellers a view of some of the most magnificent scenery in the area, including snow-capped mountains, deep green rivers, alpine meadows, and giant icefields and glaciers that are many thousands of years old.

3   Highway 93, as the Parkway is also called, begins at a cutoff on the Trans-Canada Highway and travels northward towards Mount Columbia. Rising nearly 3,750 metres into the sky, Mount Columbia is the highest point in Alberta. It is also the peak of the Columbia Icefield, the largest icefield in southern Canada. This icefield is an area of over 389 square kilometres covered in ice and snow. It is located on a ridge running along the middle of the Rocky Mountains called the Continental Divide.

4   A "divide" is a point usually located high on a mountain top where waters

begin to flow down each side of the slope. The highest point on this slope forms a natural intersection between waters that flow down one side and waters that flow down the other.

5   The Columbia Icefield covers a unique three-way divide at the boundary between British Columbia, Alberta and both Banff and Jasper Parks. Here, from the Snow Dome high up in the Columbia Icefield, the melting waters of three mighty glaciers drain in separate directions towards the Atlantic, Pacific and Arctic Oceans.

6   The rim of the Columbia Icefield can be seen from several points along the Parkway. Travellers can enjoy a clear view of spectacular icefalls and glacier ice flows creeping down mountainsides and over cliffs.

7   Goat Lookout, for example, is a point 37 kilometres south of Jasper Park. It offers a stunning view of the Athabasca Valley, where sightseers often spot wild mountain goats and bighorn sheep. Tourists can also travel the icy slopes of the Athabasca Glacier in specially designed snow-coaches that tour the area.

8   Other spectacular landmarks along the Icefields Parkway include the waterfalls and valleys created by the Sunwapta River. Beginning with the awesome view at Sunwapta Pass, where a wide green meadow opens up to reveal the snow topped peak of Mount Athabasca, the Parkway continues on towards Sunwapta Falls. Here the river plunges into a deep canyon before flowing out through beautiful forests.

9   It may not be Canada's longest highway, but nothing compares to the beauty of Alberta's Icefields Parkway.

THE MAIN IDEA

Circle the letter of the sentence which best describes the main idea of the article about the Icefield Parkway. Be prepared to support your answer.

a) Banff and Jasper National Parks.
b) What there is along the Icefields Parkway.
c) Mount Columbia: Home of the Columbia Icefield.
d) A 230 kilometre stretch of highway.

UNDERSTANDING WHAT YOU READ

If you can, answer these questions from memory. If you cannot, look back at the article.

1) What types of scenery does a person see when travelling the Icefields Parkway?

____

2) What is a "divide"?

____

3) What can travellers see at the rim of the Columbia Icefield?

____

4) What happens to the Sunwapta River at Sunwapta Falls?

____

REMEMBERING DETAILS

Write TRUE or FALSE under each statement. If the statement is false, write the statement correctly.

1) The Icefields Parkway winds its way from Lake Louise to Jasper.

____

2) Highway 66, as the Parkway is also called, begins at a cutoff on Yonge Street and travels south towards Mount Royal.

____

3) Sightseers often spot mountain lions and kangaroos at Goat Lookout.

____

4) There are many things which compare to the beauty of the Icefields Parkway.

____

INFERENCES

Based on the article, circle the letter of the best sentence completion.

1) The Icefields Parkway...

a) is often closed because of heavy snow storms.
b) can only be driven in specially designed snow-coaches.
c) goes straight across the Columbia Icefield.
d) is an important route for tourists visiting Banff and Jasper Parks.

2) The Continental Divide...

a) extends east and west across the country.
b) is part of nature.
c) runs right by Goat Lookout.
d) posed a major obstacle when building the Icefields Parkway.

INTERPRETATION

1) Using an encyclopedia, atlas or other reference material write a brief
   description of how mountains or glaciers are formed. Discuss.

2) Write a short composition about a trip out onto the Athabasca Glacier in a
   specially designed snow-coach. On this trip you meet an Abominable
   Snowman. What happens? Discuss.

3) Alone or with a partner, choose and research one of Canada's National Parks.
   Give a short speech telling the rest of the class about the park you chose.

WORD POWER

Circle the letter of the word that means the same as the word on the left.

1) stretch	a) distance	b) curve	c elevated
2) peak	a) base	b) left side	c) tip
3) flow	a) pour	b) slice	c) dice
4) creeping	a) bouncing	b) sliding	c) elevating
5) specially	a) uniquely	b) oddly	c) basically
6) plunges	a) swirls	b) spins	c) descends

FIND-THE-WORDS PUZZLE

You will find words from the article hidden in the box below. Find each word and circle all its letters. To find the words you may have to read from left-to-right, from right-to-left, upward, downward or diagonally. You should be able to find all the words given in the list below the box.

J	J	W	O	L	F	T	Y	V	G	S	M
S	A	T	R	E	B	L	A	T	L	N	O
K	P	S	L	O	P	E	W	R	A	R	U
E	S	L	P	F	F	L	K	A	C	O	N
T	L	S	R	E	V	I	R	V	I	H	T
A	L	C	C	M	R	K	A	E	E	G	A
R	A	A	I	L	V	S	P	L	R	I	I
A	F	N	J	N	I	P	Y	L	S	B	N
P	E	Y	I	C	E	F	I	E	L	D	S
E	C	O	D	A	W	C	F	R	G	W	F
S	I	N	Y	M	N	G	S	S	K	Y	F
L	O	C	A	T	E	D	F	F	N	A	B

ALBERTA	LOCATED
BANFF	MOUNTAINS
BIGHORN	PARKWAY
CANYON	RIVERS
CLIFFS	SCENIC
FLOW	SEPARATE
GLACIERS	SKY
ICEFALLS	SLOPE
ICEFIELDS	TRAVELLERS
JASPER	VIEW

ANSWER KEY

THE MAIN IDEA

b) What there is along the Icefields Parkway.

UNDERSTANDING WHAT YOU READ

1) Sights travellers see when on the Icefields Parkway include some of the most magnificent scenery in the area, including snow-capped mountains, deep green rivers, alpine meadows, and giant icefields and glaciers that are many thousands of years old.
2) A "divide" is a point usually located high on a mountain top where waters begin to flow down each side of the slope. The highest point on this slope forms a natural intersection between waters that flow down one side and waters that flow down the other.
3) Travellers to the rim of the Columbia Icefield can enjoy a clear view of spectacular icefalls and glacier ice flows creeping down mountainsides and over cliffs.
4) At Sunwapta Falls the Sunwapta River plunges into a deep canyon before flowing out through beautiful forests.

REMEMBERING DETAILS

1) T
2) F   Highway 93, as the Parkway is also called, begins at a cutoff on the Trans-Canada Highway and travels northward towards Mount Columbia.
3) F   Sightseers often spot mountain goats and bighorn sheep at Goat Lookout.
4) F   Nothing compares to the beauty of Alberta's Icefields Parkway.

INFERENCES

1) d
2) b

WORD POWER

1) a
2) c
3) a
4) b
5) a
6) c

FIND-THE-WORDS PUZZLE

```
J     W  O  L  F        Y        G        M
   A  T  R  E  B  L  A  T     L     N     O
      S  L  O  P  E  W     R     A     R  U
E  S     P           K  A     C     O     N
T  L  S  R  E  V  I  R  V     I     H     T
A  L  C  C        R     A  E     E     G  A
R  A  A  I  L  V     P     L     R  I     I
A  F  N     N  I           L     S  B     N
P  E  Y  I  C  E  F  I  E  L  D        S
E  C  O        W  C  F  R
S  I  N           S  S  K  Y
L  O  C  A  T  E  D  F  F  N  A  B
```

J: James Bay Project

1   In 1971, a large convoy of trucks and bulldozers began cutting a path through the wilderness of northern Quebec en route to the James Bay area. They were part of the construction team hired to build the largest, costliest and most ambitious energy project the world had ever seen, the James Bay Project.

2   The James Bay Project involved building a series of huge power plants by first damming the rivers that flow into James Bay. But in the years since the rumble of construction crews was first heard in the area, the James Bay hydro-electric project has been generating both electricity -- and controversy.

Of all the water found in Canada's   3 rivers, a full one-third of it flows through rivers that drain into the James Bay/Hudson Bay region of the Quebec/Labrador Peninsula. Power companies had long recognized the huge potential these waters held for generating electricity. However, Quebec's giant utility Hydro-Quebec was the first company to tap this potential by launching the James Bay Project.

The three-phase plan called for the   4 eventual construction of 36 dams and thousands of dikes on 20 rivers running through northern Quebec. The first phase of the project centred on La Grande River, an 800 kilometre

waterway with headwaters in the
northern highlands of the peninsula.

5   When construction began in 1971,
the cost of La Grande Phase 1 was
estimated to be six billion dollars. By
the time it was completed in 1985, the
cost had risen to somewhere between
sixteen and twenty billion dollars.
Much of this was spent on building
206 dikes and nine dams, the tallest of
which stood as high as a 50-storey
building.

6   Supporters of the James Bay Project
argued that its true value could not be
measured in dollars, since it guaranteed
the Province of Quebec an endless
supply of energy and wealth well into
the future. However, there were many
people who opposed the project from
the very beginning, starting with Native
groups who lived in the area.

7   None of the approximately 5,000
Cree and 3,500 Inuit who lived in
northern Quebec were warned their
Native homeland would be lost forever

once the James Bay Project was
completed. As well, environmental
groups claimed the project was an
ecological disaster equal to the
destruction of the rainforests, since
thousands of square kilometres of
natural waterways and forests would
wind up flooded and under water.

Although both Native and   8
environmental groups rallied against
the project, the signing of the James
Bay and Northern Quebec agreement
in 1975 gave Hydro-Quebec the right
to continue construction. This
agreement saw Native groups sign
away their aboriginal right to the land
in exchange for money, other land and
the right to govern their own affairs.

With plans for further construction   9
scheduled right into the next century,
the James Bay Project continues to
grow in size. However, with each new
development, another piece of
Quebec's beautiful northern wilderness
disappears forever.

THE MAIN IDEA

Circle the letter of the sentence which best describes the main idea of the article
about the James Bay Project. Be prepared to support your answer.

a) The unexpected result of hydro-electric projects.
b) The La Grande phase of the James Bay Project.
c) The true value of the James Bay Project.
d) The James Bay Project: Home of electricity and controversy.

UNDERSTANDING WHAT YOU READ

If you can, answer these questions from memory. If you cannot, look back at the article.

1) What did construction of the James Bay Project involve?

____

2) How much money was the La Grande Phase 1 estimated to cost? By the time it was finished, how much did it cost?

____

3) What value did supporters of the James Bay Project give it?

____

4) What happens with each new addition to the James Bay Project?

____

REMEMBERING DETAILS

Write TRUE or FALSE under each statement. If the statement is false, write the statement correctly.

1) One third of all the water found in Canada's rivers flows into the James Bay/Hudson Bay region.

____

2) Not many people opposed the James Bay Project.

____

3) The Cree and Inuit who lived in northern Quebec were given plenty of warning as to what the results would be if the James Bay Project was constructed.

____

4) The Native groups were never given anything when they signed away their aboriginal right to the land around the James Bay Project.

____

INFERENCES

Based on the article, circle the letter of the best sentence completion.

1) The James Bay Project...

a) has a good side and a bad side.
b) was designed by some of the world's top engineers.
c) was completed in 1971.
d) is as high as a 50-storey building.

2) The people of Quebec...

a) do not care about the damage done to the northern regions of their province.
b) pay less for their hydro-electricity than people in other provinces.
c) want construction halted on further expansion to the James Bay Project.
d) benefit from the project by having plenty of electricity.

INTERPRETATION

1) Break the class into four groups: one group representing Hydro-Quebec, one group representing the Native groups, one group representing supporters of the project and, finally, one group representing those people opposed to the project. With your group, prepare your argument for or against the project. Debate the issue.

2) Besides the people affected by the hydro-electric project, consider nature. Prepare an environmental impact statement detailing what effect such a construction would have on the plants and animals in the area. Discuss.

3) Write a short composition describing what it would be like if tomorrow you woke up and there was no electricity, ever again! What would life be like?

WORD POWER

Circle the letter of the word that means the same as the word on the left.

1) convoy	a) fleet	b) shipment	c) edifice
2) series	a) congestion	b) playoff	c) string
3) controversy	a) expense	b) debate	c) absolution
4) tap	a) spill	b) promote	c) draw off
5) endless	a) undying	b) insurmountable	c) dainty
6) affairs	a) leaders	b) business	c) considerations

FIND-THE-WORDS PUZZLE

You will find words from the article hidden in the box below. Find each word and
circle all its letters. To find the words you may have to read from left-to-right,
from right-to-left, upward, downward or diagonally. You should be able to find all
the words given in the list below the box.

```
S   I   Z   E   D   S   S   E   K   I   D   R
Y   I   W   F   W   A   V   C   A   E   R   A
T   M   G   E   L   D   M   P   S   B   K   L
I   A   R   N   R   O   E   S   P   K   S   L
C   C   T   E   S   A   K   D   U   U   D   I
I   L   A   I   T   N   E   T   O   P   N   E
R   I   G   H   T   Z   L   I   R   O   A   D
T   F   O   R   E   S   T   S   G   H   L   V
C   O   S   T   L   I   E   S   T   C   H   F
E   Y   I   E   B   T   O   P   C   Z   G   D
L   R   U   M   B   L   E   D   E   R   I   H
E   V   A   L   U   E   M   P   A   T   H   S
```

AMBITIOUS	HIGHLANDS
AREA	HIRED
COSTLIEST	PATH
CREWS	POTENTIAL
DAMS	RALLIED
DIKES	RIGHT
ELECTRICITY	RUMBLE
FLOODED	SIGNS
FORESTS	SIZE
GROUPS	VALUE

ANSWER KEY

THE MAIN IDEA

d) The James Bay Project: Home of electricity and controversy.

UNDERSTANDING WHAT YOU READ

1) Construction of the James Bay Project involved building a series of huge power plants. This was first done by damming the rivers that flow into James Bay. The three-phase plan called for the eventual construction of 36 dams and thousands of dikes on 20 rivers running through northern Quebec.
2) When construction began in 1971, the cost of La Grande Phase 1 was estimated to be six billion dollars. By the time it was completed in 1985, the cost had risen to somewhere between sixteen and twenty billion dollars.
3) Supporters of the James Bay Project argued that its true value could not be measured in dollars since it guaranteed the Province of Quebec an endless supply of energy and wealth well into the future.
4) With each new addition to the James Bay Project another, piece of Quebec's beautiful northern wilderness disappears forever.

REMEMBERING DETAILS

1) T
2) F   There were many people who opposed the project from the very beginning, starting with Native groups who lived in the area.
3) F   None of the approximately 5,000 Cree and 3,500 Inuit who lived in northern Quebec were warned their Native homeland would be lost forever once the James Bay Project was completed.
4) F   The Native groups were given money, land and the right to govern their own affairs in exchange for signing away their aboriginal right to the land near the James Bay Project.

INFERENCES

1) a
2) d

WORD POWER

1) a
2) c
3) b
4) c
5) a
6) b

FIND-THE-WORDS PUZZLE

S	I	Z	E	D	S	S	E	K	I	D	R
Y	I			W	A			A	E	R	A
T		G	E		D	M		S			L
I		R	N			E	S	P		S	L
C	C			S			D	U	U	D	I
I	L	A	I	T	N	E	T	O	P	N	E
R	I	G	H	T			I	R	O	A	D
T	F	O	R	E	S	T	S	G		L	
C	O	S	T	L	I	E	S	T		H	F
E				B						G	
L	R	U	M	B	L	E	D	E	R	I	H
E	V	A	L	U	E			P	A	T	H

J6

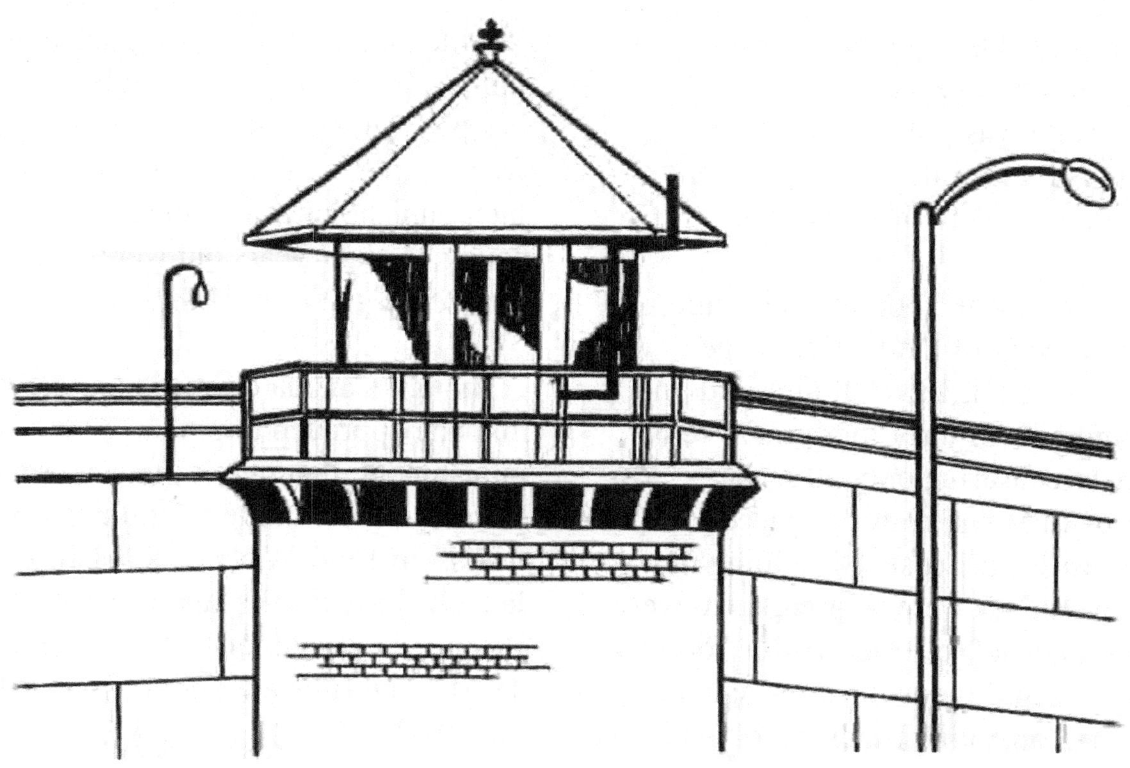

K: Kingston Penitentiary

1   It's been said that "laws are made to be broken." But for people who break the laws, there has always been the threat of being punished. For thousands of Canadian criminals, this punishment has often meant being locked away behind the brick walls and steel bars of Canada's oldest provincial prison, Kingston Penitentiary.

2   Long before Confederation brought Canada's original provinces together in 1867, Kingston Penitentiary was being used to house the country's men and women convicted of crime. Designed by architect William Coverdale and built in 1835, Kingston Penitentiary is a lasting symbol of Canada's response to crime and punishment.

3   The idea for a provincial penitentiary was first suggested in the House of Assembly of Upper Canada as early as 1826. Public concern over the increasing crime rate in Canada's rapidly growing cities helped support the plan. Until that point, criminals were often sentenced to endure corporal punishment -- physical penalties such as whipping or strapping. More often they were packed into tiny, overcrowded jails and left to fend for themselves amidst the sometimes violent prison population.

4   After studying the success of the penitentiary system in both England and the United States, officials decided to build Canada's first penitentiary. Although Hamilton was originally

considered as a possible location, consruction began at Hatter's Bay. This site was a short walk from Kingston near the village of Portsmouth on Lake Ontario.

5   Using local labourers. the original south wing of the Kingston "pen" was completed in 1834. It included one hundred and forty four prison cells, each measuring only 30 inches -- less than 100 centimetres -- wide. However, the costs of building the penitentiary were so great there were no funds left over to provide food and guards at the prison, and it sat empty. When operating funds were finally set aside for the prison, Kingston Penitentiary received its first six prisoners on June 1, 1835.

6   Over the years, changes at Kingston Penitentiary have reflected the changes in Canada's approach to criminal justice. For example, early life in Kingston Penitentiary was harsh and brutal for prisoners. Beatings were considered a part of prison punishment, and guilty inmates were regularly stripped, buckled down and strapped. Women and children were not spared such punishment, and convicts as young as eight years old were reportedly given the lash.

7   Though Canada developed a more humane approach to prison punishment, that didn't prevent crime from being committed within prison walls. In 1836, Alberzy Nakusilio launched the first escape attempt. The first guard was killed at the prison in 1870. And riots erupted in 1932, 1954 and 1971.

8   Today modern facilities like Millhaven Penitentiary have reduced the flow of Canada's most dangerous and notorious criminals to Kingston. But despite being over 160 years old, Kingston Penitentiary continues to serve an important role in Canada's correctional service.

THE MAIN IDEA

Circle the letter of the sentence which best describes the main idea of the article about Kingston Penitentiary. Be prepared to support your answer.

a) Prison reform in Canada.
b) Canada's oldest provincial prison.
c) The need for new prisons.
d) The history of corporal punishment in Canada.

UNDERSTANDING WHAT YOU READ

If you can, answer these questions from memory. If you cannot, look back at the article.

1) What helped support the idea to build a provincial penitentiary?

2) Why, after it was finished being built, did the penitentiary sit empty?

3) In the early days of the Kingston Penitentiary, what was life like for the prisoners?

4) Is the Kingston Penitentiary still being used today?

REMEMBERING DETAILS

Write TRUE or FALSE under each statement. If the statement is false, write the statement correctly.

1) Before 1867, Kingston Penitentiary was being used as a resort hotel.

2) Canadian officials went ahead and built Kingston Penitentiary without doing any research into how prisons were being built and run in other countries.

3) Massages were considered a part of prison punishment, and guilty inmates were regularly stripped and massaged from head to toe.

4) Modern facilities like Millhaven Penitentiary have reduced the flow of Canada's most dangerous and notorious criminals into Kingston.

INFERENCES

Based on the article, circle the letter of the best sentence completion.

1) The fact that the prison was built even before Confederation...

a) shows that government officials were thinking ahead.
b) proves that crime has been a problem since before the country officially began.
c) leads one to believe the police were not doing their job back then.
d) could be because convicts were set free in other countries and sent to Canada.

2) In the over 160 years the Kingston Penitentiary has existed...

a) public concern over crime has diminished.
b) hundreds of convicts have escaped.
c) no renovations have ever been done to the building.
d) there have always been criminals.

INTERPRETATION

1) Today, modern prisons do not use corporal punishment as much as they used
   to. Do you think corporal punishment should be brought back as a deterrent to
   crime? What about capital punishment?

2) Conduct a poll. As a class devise a questionnaire about crime and prison
   issues. Then, go out and ask a variety of different people your questions.
   Combine your results to produce some statistics.

3) Write a short composition about a day in the life of a prisoner in the Kingston
   Penitentiary in the early days of the facility.

WORD POWER

Circle the letter of the word that means the same as the word on the left.

1) endure	a) spend	b) realize	c) suffer
2) fend	a) strive	b) muscle	c) protect
3) amidst	a) among	b) against	c) besides
4) lash	a) bind	b) whip	c) stick
5) attempt	a) failure	b) try	c) prevention
6) facilities	a) committees	b) sheds	c) buildings

FIND-THE-WORDS PUZZLE

You will find words from the article hidden in the box below. Find each word and
circle all its letters. To find the words you may have to read from left-to-right,
from right-to-left, upward, downward or diagonally. You should be able to find all
the words given in the list below the box.

```
S  G  N  I  T  A  E  B  H  M  C  N
P  U  N  I  S  H  E  D  S  E  O  O
E  A  R  C  H  I  T  E  C  T  N  S
N  R  K  R  C  B  N  K  O  S  S  I
A  D  L  A  G  R  C  R  E  Y  T  R
L  S  C  G  C  V  I  N  N  S  R  P
T  W  U  E  S  O  E  M  W  Y  U  M
I  A  L  R  U  M  O  K  E  E  C  E
E  L  A  S  O  F  U  N  D  S  T  N
S  B  Y  W  N  O  T  S  G  N  I  K
L  A  B  O  U  R  E  R  S  T  O  S
N  Y  H  S  R  A  H  U  M  A  N  E
```

ARCHITECT	KINGSTON
BARS	LABOURERS
BEATINGS	LAWS
CELLS	MEN
CONSTRUCTION	NOTORIOUS
CRIME	PENALTIES
FUNDS	PRISON
GUARDS	PUNISHED
HARSH	SYSTEM
HUMANE	WOMEN

ANSWER KEY

THE MAIN IDEA

b) Canada's oldest provincial prison.

UNDERSTANDING WHAT YOU READ

1 Public concern over the increasing crime rate in Canada's rapidly growing cities helped support the idea of building a provincial penitentiary.
2 The costs of building the penitentiary were so great there were no funds left over to provide food and guards at the prison, so the prison sat empty.
3) Early life in Kingston Penitentiary was harsh and brutal for prisoners. Beatings were considered a part of prison punishment, and guilty inmates were regularly stripped, buckled down and strapped. Women and children were not spared such punishment, and convicts as young as eight years old were reportedly give the lash.
4) Despite being over 160 years old, Kingston Penitentiary is still being used and continues to serve an important role in Canada's correctional service.

REMEMBERING DETAILS

1) F   By 1867, Kingston Penitentiary was being used to house the country's men and women convicted of crime.
2) F   Only after studying the success of the penitentiary systems in both England and the United States did Canadian officials decide to build the Kingston Penitentiary.
3) F   Beatings were considered a part of prison punishment, and guilty inmates were regularly stripped, buckled down and strapped.
4) T

INFERENCES

1) b
2) d

WORD POWER

1) c
2) c
3) a
4) b
5) b
6) c

FIND-THE-WORDS PUZZLE

S	G	N	I	T	A	E	B		M	C	N
P	U	N	I	S	H	E	D		E	O	O
E	A	R	C	H	I	T	E	C	T	N	S
N	R			C				O	S	S	I
A	D			R		R			Y	T	R
L	S			C		I	N		S	R	P
T	W		E	S	O	E	M			U	M
I	A	L	R	U	M			E		C	E
E	L	A	S	O	F	U	N	D	S	T	N
S	B		W	N	O	T	S	G	N	I	K
L	A	B	O	U	R	E	R	S		O	
		H	S	R	A	H	U	M	A	N	E

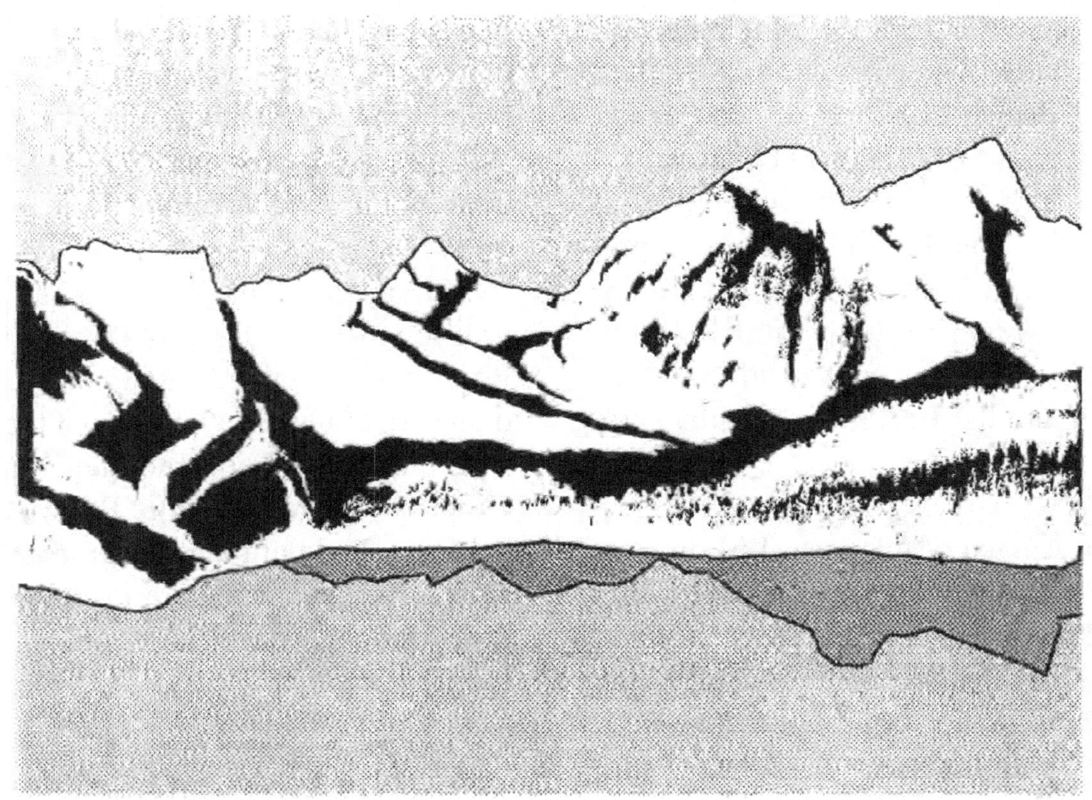

L: Lake Louise

1   If a contest were held to determine the most beautiful place on earth, Lake Louise would certainly be a strong contender.

2   Once an isolated lake in the Canadian Rocky Mountains known only to local Indians, Lake Louise has since become one of the most recognizable landmarks in Canada. Its image has appeared in literally thousands of advertisements, photographs, movies, postcards and paintings. Over 100 million people have visited the tiny lake since its discovery, and another 1.6 million visit each year. With the area's scenic view unmatched anywhere else in Canada, it is easy to see why.

3   Surrounded by snowcapped mountains and fed by icy glaciers, Lake Louise is like a hidden treasure buried deep in the mountains of Banff National Park in southwest Alberta. With its almost turquoise-coloured waters resting silently in the shadow of Mount Victoria and the Victoria Glacier, Lake Louise has been called the "most beautiful lake in the Western hemisphere."

4   Although it has become a favourite destination for tourists from around the world, no one but local Indians had visited the area before 1882. That was the year a former Northwest Mounted Police officer named Thomas "Tom" Edmund Wilson became the first white man to set his eyes on the lake.

5   The fact that Wilson was even near

the area was the result of a long series of events. These began in 1870, the year British Columbia joined Canada. Government officials in Ottawa promised to the new province that a railway would be built within 10 years to connect British Columbia to the rest of the country. Though the project was delayed, railway crews had made their way into the B.C. mountains by spring 1882.

6   In August of that year, Wilson was part of a crew surveying land for the railway. One night as he sat around a campfire with a small group of Stoney Indians, Wilson could hear the thundering roar of avalanches coming from high up in the mountains. According to an Indian guide named Edwin the Gold Seeker, the thunder came from a great white mountain located above a body of water the Stoneys called "Lake of Little Fishes."

7   The next morning, Wilson and the

guide travelled up the slope and discovered a beautiful sheet of deep blue water as smooth as a mirror. Wilson gave it the name "Emerald Lake," and word about the discovery quickly spread across the country. In 1884, Emerald Lake became Lake Louise when it was renamed after Princess Caroline Alberta Louise, daughter of Queen Victoria and the wife of Canada's governor general. By 1890 the Canadian Pacific Railway company had built a beautiful chateau beside the lake, and Lake Louise soon grew into one of the most popular tourist resorts in Canada.

8   With depths of up to 75 metres, the water temperature of Lake Louise barely rises above freezing. But there's no question the natural splendor of Lake Louise gives everyone who visits there a warm feeling and a lifetime of memories.

THE MAIN IDEA

Circle the letter of the sentence which best describes the main idea of the article about Lake Louise. Be prepared to support your answer.

a) The renaming of Emerald Lake.
b) A lifetime of memories.
c) Tom Wilson meets Edwin the Gold Seeker.
d) A tiny, turquoise-coloured lake visited by millions of people.

UNDERSTANDING WHAT YOU READ

If you can, answer these questions from memory. If you cannot, look back at the article.

1) Where has Lake Louise's image appeared?

____

2) Who was the first white man to set eyes on Lake Louise?

____

3) What did government officials in Ottawa promise to the new province of British Columbia?

____

4) Who is Lake Louise named after?

____

REMEMBERING DETAILS

Write TRUE or FALSE under each statement. If the statement is false, write the statement correctly.

1) Lake Louise was once only known to local Indians.

____

2) Lake Louise has also been known as The Lake of Big Fish and Blue Lake.

____

3) Sitting around a campfire, Tom Wilson could hear a waterfall from below in the valley.

____

4) Lake Louise is shallow and the water is always warm enough for swimming.

____

INFERENCES

Based on the article, circle the letter of the best sentence completion.

1) After being led to the lake by his Indian guide, Tom Wilson...

a) knew why the Indians called it Lake of Little Fishes.
b) realized the railway could never pass near there.
c) claimed the land for the government of Canada.
d) thought the lake was so beautiful he started telling people about it.

2) The Canadian Pacific Railway...

a) purposely delayed construction of the railway into British Columbia.
b) recognized the tourist potential of Lake Louise immediately.
c) has stopped passenger train operations around Lake Louise.
d) did not want the name Emerald Lake changed.

INTERPRETATION

1) For many people Lake Louise is the most beautiful place in the world. Have
   you ever visited Lake Louise? If yes, do you agree that it is the most
   beautiful? Describe and discuss the most beautiful place in the world you have
   visited.

2) What are some other places in Canada and around the world that are very
   beautiful? List ten. Discuss.

3) At this point in time our planet has been explored from north to south and from
   east to west. Imagine you are the person who discovers a place on earth that
   has yet to be seen by any other human. In a short composition, describe the
   place you discovered and how you discovered it.

WORD POWER

Circle the letter of the word that means the same as the word on the left.

1) contender	a) challenger	b) acquisition	c) momento
2) unmatched	a) unopened	b) uneven	c) unequalled
3) local	a) nomadic	b) nearby	c) plains
4) former	a) respected	b) onetime	c) humiliated
5) guide	a) soldier	b) tourist	c) escort
6) barely	a) hardly	b) constantly	c) gradually

FIND-THE-WORDS PUZZLE

You will find words from the article hidden in the box below. Find each word and circle all its letters. To find the words you may have to read from left-to-right, from right-to-left, upward, downward or diagonally. You should be able to find all the words given in the list below the box.

```
S   G   R   B   D   S   P   R   E   A   D   C
L   N   M   R   E   R   H   S   Y   E   W   E
O   I   S   O   L   A   T   E   D   N   T   M
P   Y   P   D   A   I   U   F   F   E   I   I
E   E   K   N   Y   L   S   T   E   I   B   T
S   V   R   E   E   W   A   H   I   H   W   E
T   R   O   L   D   A   S   K   T   F   C   F
R   U   R   P   H   Y   P   R   E   Y   U   I
O   S   R   S   K   R   A   M   D   N   A   L
S   H   I   D   B   E   W   O   D   A   H   S
E   T   M   C   O   N   N   E   C   T   G   W
R   A   V   A   L   A   N   C   H   E   S   A
```

AVALANCHES	RAILWAY
BEAUTIFUL	RESORTS
CONNECT	SHADOW
DELAYED	SHEET
EARTH	SLOPE
ISOLATED	SPLENDOR
LAKE	SPREAD
LANDMARKS	SURVEYING
LIFETIME	TINY
MIRROR	WIFE

ANSWER KEY

THE MAIN IDEA

d) A tiny, turquoise-coloured lake visited by millions of people.

UNDERSTANDING WHAT YOU READ

1) Lake Louise's image has appeared in literally thousands of advertisements, photographs, movies, postcards and paintings.
2) Thomas "Tom" Edmund Wilson was the first white man to set eyes on Lake Louise.
3) Government officials in Ottawa promised the new province of British Columbia that a railway would be built within 10 years to connect British Columbia to the rest of the country.
4) Lake Louise was named after Princess Caroline Alberta Louise, daughter of Queen Victoria and the wife of Canada's governor general.

REMEMBERING DETAILS

1) T
2) F   Lake Louise has also been known as Lake of the Little Fishes and Emerald Lake.
3) F   Sitting around a campfire, Wilson could hear the thundering roar of avalanches coming from high up in the mountains.
4) F   With depths of up to 75 metres, the water temperature of Lake Louise barely rises above freezing. This would be a little cold for swimming!

INFERENCES

1) d
2) h

WORD POWER

1) a
2) c
3) b
4) b
5) c
6) a

FIND-THE-WORDS PUZZLE

```
S  G     B  D  S  P  R  E  A  D
L  N     R  E  R           Y        E
O  I  S  O  L  A  T  E  D  N  T  M
P  Y     D  A  I  U        F  E  I  I
E  E     N  Y  L     T  E  I     T
S  V  R  E  E  W  A  H  I  H  W  E
T  R  O  L  D  A  S  K  T  F     F
R  U  R  P     Y     R  E     U  I
O  S  R  S  K  R  A  M  D  N  A  L
S     I        E  W  O  D  A  H  S
E     M  C  O  N  N  E  C  T
R  A  V  A  L  A  N  C  H  E  S
```

M: Manitoulin Island

1   Although there are many different views on the subject, no one can say for certain exactly how the earth was formed. But according to local Indian legend, there's no question that the Great Spirit "Kitche Manitou" is the creator of one of Canada's most beautiful landmarks, Manitoulin Island.

2   Located in the northern waters of Lake Huron in Ontario, Manitoulin Island is the largest freshwater island in the world. Measuring nearly 130 kilometres long and from 4 to 48 kilometres wide, Manitoulin is the largest in a series of islands known in geographic terms as an "archipelago."

3   This formation is part of the famous Niagara Escarpment, a high ridge of land that begins in the United States and extends north along the Bruce Peninsula and on towards the Manitoulin area. The island's east coast combines with the Bruce Peninsula to help form Georgian Bay. This giant body of fresh water off lake Huron's northeastern shores was once known as Lake Manitoulin.

4   The name Manitoulin is taken from local Indian languages. Translated into English, it means "Spirit Island." The island is believed to be the sacred home of the Great Spirit Kitche Manitou, the creator of heaven and earth.

5   According to legend, Manitoulin Island was a special project of Kitche Manitou. After completing the world,

the Spirit took the very best parts of Creation and combined them into an island paradise set in an inland sea. These elements included the purest waters, the bluest skies, the greenest forests and the brightest clouds. Once the island was attached to the earth, he named it "Manitou-miniss," or Island of Manitou.

well. By the 1870s, settlements had arisen at such places as Gore Bay, Providence Bay, Little Current and Manitowaning. Today the island remains a spiritual homeland rich in Native history, but as well it is a thriving community shared equally by the ancestors of both Native and European settlers.

6   The first non-Native to visit the island was a Jesuit priest named Father Joseph Poncet, who was sent there in 1648 to build a Catholic mission. Father Poncet and many of the local Indians were eventually forced to flee both the mission and the island following a series of violent raids by Iroquois Indians in 1650.

7   Although a treaty with the Canadian government in 1836 gave Native groups the sole right to settle on Manitoulin, a treaty signed in 1862 opened the island up to non-Natives as

Manitoulin Island is also a favourite 8 destination for travellers despite its isolated location. Whether they arrive via the Trans-Canada Highway in the north, or by ferry-boat from Tobermory in the south, tourists travelling to Manitoulin Island can enjoy some of the most beautiful scenery in Canada.

From the delicate waters of Bridal 9 Veil Falls to the sweeping sands of Providence Bay, Manitoulin Island is not only the world's largest freshwater island, it is also one of the most enjoyable places to visit.

THE MAIN IDEA

Circle the letter of the sentence which best describes the main idea of the article about Manitoulin Island. Be prepared to support your answer.

a) The forming of Georgian Bay.
b) Kitche Manitou: the Great Spirit.
c) An enjoyable place to visit.
d) Spirit Island.

UNDERSTANDING WHAT YOU READ

If you can, answer these questions from memory. If you cannot, look back at the article.

1) According to local Indian legend, who created Manitoulin Island?

____

2) When translated into English, what does Manitoulin mean?

____

3) What parts of Creation were combined to form Manitoulin Island?

____

4) What did the treaty signed in 1862 reverse from an earlier treaty signed in
   1836?

____

REMEMBERING DETAILS

Write TRUE or FALSE under each statement. If the statement is false, write the statement correctly.

1) Scientists know exactly how the earth was formed.

____

2) The first non-Native to visit Manitoulin Island was a surveyor for the Canadian
   Pacific Railway named Tom Wilson.

____

3) Today much of the Native history which made Manitoulin Island a spiritual
   homeland has been forgotten.

____

4) Manitoulin Island is the world's largest freshwater island.

____

INFERENCES

Based on the article, circle the letter of the best sentence completion.

1) Realizing that Manitoulin Island is in an archipelago...

a) is proof that it was created by a Great Spirit.
b) lets us know that there are other islands nearby.
c) makes it obvious that you can only get there by bridge or ferry-boat.
d) shows that it is sacred.

2) Father Poncet was sent to Manitoulin Island...

a) to convert the Natives to Catholicism.
b) to be a link in the fur trade.
c) to study Native hunting and fishing techniques.
d) to learn all about Kitche Manitou.

INTERPRETATION

1) The world's many religions have a great deal in common. Discuss.

2) Imagine you are Father Poncet and you have just seen Manitoulin Island for the
first time. Write a letter to your friends back in Europe describing your first
impressions.

3) Write a short composition describing the creation of Manitoulin Island.

WORD POWER

Circle the letter of the word that means the same as the word on the left.

1) for certain	a) indefinitely	b) for sure	c) chronologically
2) extends	a) wavers	b) elevates	c) stretches
3) flee	a) leave	b) rebuild	c) organize
4) thriving	a) prosperous	b) quaint	c) tiny
5) despite	a) looking for	b) because of	c) regardless of
6) delicate	a) raging	b) gentle	c) dripping

FIND-THE-WORDS PUZZLE

You will find words from the article hidden in the box below. Find each word and circle all its letters. To find the words you may have to read from left-to-right, from right-to-left, upward, downward or diagonally. You should be able to find all the words given in the list below the box.

```
S  P  I  R  I  T  U  A  L  R  O  B
A  T  H  E  A  V  E  N  B  I  R  R
C  R  S  T  L  I  P  C  L  D  O  I
R  A  D  E  R  O  D  E  U  G  T  G
E  N  N  B  N  A  S  S  E  E  A  H
D  S  A  T  L  E  E  T  S  P  E  T
D  L  L  I  S  W  E  O  T  F  R  E
E  A  E  S  I  D  A  R  A  P  C  S
M  T  M  I  V  F  N  S  G  S  I  T
R  E  O  V  G  B  T  A  I  F  V  S
O  D  H  F  A  M  O  U  S  D  H  C
F  O  G  A  L  E  P  I  H  C  R  A
```

ANCESTORS	HOMELAND
ARCHIPELAGO	PARADISE
BLUEST	RAIDS
BRIGHTEST	RIDGE
CREATOR	SACRED
EARTH	SANDS
FAMOUS	SOLE
FORMED	SPIRITUAL
GREENEST	TRANSLATED
HEAVEN	VISIT

ANSWER KEY

THE MAIN IDEA

d) Spirit Island.

UNDERSTANDING WHAT YOU READ

1) According to local Indian legend, the Great Spirit "Kitche Manitou" is the creator of Manitoulin Island.
2) When translated into English, it means "Spirit Island."
3) The very best parts of Creation were combined to form Manitoulin Island. These elements included the purest waters, the bluest skies, the greenest forests and the brightest clouds.
4) The treaty signed in 1862 opened the island up to non-Natives as well as to Natives. The treaty in 1836 had given Native groups the sole right to settle on Manitoulin.

REMEMBERING DETAILS

1) F   No one can say for certain exactly how the earth was formed.
2) F   The first non-Native to visit the island was a Jesuit priest named Father Joseph Poncet, who was sent there in 1648 to build a Catholic mission.
3) F   Today the island remains a spiritual homeland rich in Native history,
4) T

INFERENCES

1) b
2) a

WORD POWER

1) b
2) c
3) a
4) a
5) c
6) b

FIND-THE-WORDS PUZZLE

S	P	I	R	I	T	U	A	L	R		B
A	T	H	E	A	V	E	N	B	I	R	R
C	R	S	T	L	I		C	L	D	O	I
R	A	D	E	R	O	D	E	U	G	T	G
E	N	N		N	A	S	S	E	E	A	H
D	S	A	T			E	E	T	S		T
D	L	L	I	S		E	O	T		R	E
E	A	E	S	I	D	A	R	A	P	C	S
M	T	M	I			N	S	G			T
R	E	O	V				A				
O	D	H	F	A	M	O	U	S			
F	Q	G	A	L	E	P	I	H	C	R	A

N: Niagara Falls

1   Kings and Queens. Presidents and Prime Ministers. Movie stars and artists. Daredevils and thrill-seekers. Newly-married couples and curious sightseers. From across North America and around the world, these are just a few of the millions of people who have travelled to Niagara Falls to see the world's most famous waterfall.

2   Standing just 58 metres high, Niagara Falls is not even one of the Top 10 highest waterfalls in North America. But it is easily one of the most powerful. One-fifth of all the fresh water in the world pours over the edge of the falls, as it flows down the river from the four upper Great Lakes: Lake Superior, Lake Huron, Lake Michigan and Lake Erie.

3   Niagara Falls is located nearly half-way down the Niagara River on the international boundary separating New York State and Ontario. The river is split by tiny Goat Island before dropping over two giant falls or "cataracts:" the smaller American Falls, and the larger Canadian Falls. The Canadian waterfall is often called the Horseshoe Falls, because its rounded U-shape looks like a giant horseshoe. The American Falls is also split in two, forming one major waterfall and a smaller "cascade" called Bridal Veil Falls.

4   Before the arrival of Europeans to the region, the Niagara River was a major trade route for Indians. Much of the folklore surrounding Niagara Falls

comes from Indian legends. For example, local Neutral Indians considered the falls a sacred place. They believed a great spirit lived in a cave behind the falls. The word "Niagara" comes from the Indian word "Ohguiaahra" meaning "the Great Thunderer." This was the name the Neutrals gave to the spirit.

5   Another story involves the legend of Lelawalo, an Indian princess who became known as the "Maid of The Mist." She was set adrift in a canoe and sent over the falls as a sacrifice. According to legend, Lelawalo returned as a spirit, and can still be seen rising through the mists at the bottom of the falls.

6   While Indians may have worshiped the falls, some early visitors feared its powerful waters. One such person was Father Louis Hennepin, a priest from the Spanish Netherlands. He is believed to be the first European to leave a written record of his trip to the Falls. Upon reaching the site for the first time in 1678, he wrote, "When one stands near the falls and looks down, one is seized with horror."

7   That warning hasn't stopped the many daredevils who have come to the falls seeking fame and fortune by performing dangerous stunts. The most famous was The Great Blondin, a tightrope walker who first crossed the river's giant gorge in 1859. A school teacher named Annie Edson Taylor was the first person to tumble over the falls in a barrel. She survived the trip on October 24, 1901, but died penniless just 20 years later.

8   Today the scenic beauty of the falls helps draw over 12 million people a year to the area. It's one reason why Niagara Falls has become the Honeymoon Capital of the World.

THE MAIN IDEA

Circle the letter of the sentence which best describes the main idea of the article about Niagara Falls. Be prepared to support your answer.

a) The Maid of The Mist.
b) The Niagara River: a natural boundary between New York State and Ontario.
c) 12 million tourists cannot be wrong.
d) The world's most famous waterfall.

UNDERSTANDING WHAT YOU READ

If you can, answer these questions from memory. If you cannot, look back at the article.

1) What kinds of people visit Niagara Falls?

____

2) Where is Niagara Falls located?

____

3) Who was Lelawalo? What happened to her?

____

4) Who was the first person to go over the falls in a barrel?

____

REMEMBERING DETAILS

Write TRUE or FALSE under each statement. If the statement is false, write the statement correctly.

1) Niagara Falls is the highest waterfall in the world.

____

2) The Canadian waterfall is often called the Horseshoe Falls because it is shaped like a giant horseshoe.

____

3) The word "Niagara" comes from the Indian word "Ohguiaahra" meaning "the Massive Rainfall."

____

4) The Great Blondin drove his rocket-equipped motorcycle across the gorge in 1989.

____

INFERENCES

Based on the article, circle the letter of the best sentence completion.

1) The power of Niagara Falls...

a) is used to generate hydro-electric power.
b) has influenced Indian myth and legends.
c) has attracted many weirdos.
d) can be overcome with a properly designed barrel.

2) Going over Niagara Falls in a barrel...

a) is a horrifying experience.
b) is worth risking the dangers involved.
c) is now impossible because a net has been installed across the width of the river.
d) does not guarantee you will be rich for the rest of your life.

INTERPRETATION

1) What do you think is the fascination that Niagara Falls has over people? Why does it draw so many tourists?

2) Would you be willing to go over Niagara Falls in a barrel? Why would you? Why not? Would you do it for one million dollars? Discuss.

3) Write a short composition from the point of view of someone inside a barrel about to plunge over Niagara Falls, or from the point of view of someone on a tightrope over Niagara Falls. What would go through that person's mind?

WORD POWER

Circle the letter of the word that means the same as the word on the left.

1) curious	a) irritable	b) interested	c) rabid
2) legend	a) trial	b) story	c) fib
3) maid	a) captain	b) fog	c) girl
4) sacrifice	a) offering	b) idol	c) mercy
5) tumble	a) jostle	b) go down	c) sprinkle
6) penniless	a) well known	b) irritated	c) broke

FIND-THE-WORDS PUZZLE

You will find words from the article hidden in the box below. Find each word and
circle all its letters. To find the words you may have to read from left-to-right,
from right-to-left, upward, downward or diagonally. You should be able to find all
the words given in the list below the box.

```
H   E   N   U   T   R   O   F   M   V   E   F
T   O   C   R   E   P   P   U   I   P   F   O
E   I   R   M   G   F   A   L   L   S   G   L
P   B   A   R   R   E   L   K   L   M   N   K
O   F   D   O   O   H   B   I   I   A   I   L
R   W   R   U   F   R   V   K   O   J   T   O
T   V   I   T   S   E   G   R   N   O   A   R
H   E   F   E   D   A   D   O   S   R   R   E
G   O   T   E   L   D   T   Y   R   H   A   V
I   N   R   N   O   I   G   E   R   G   P   A
T   A   F   F   M   I   S   T   C   O   E   C
D   C   A   T   A   R   A   C   T   S   S   B
```

ADRIFT	GORGE
BARREL	HORROR
CANOE	MAJOR
CATARACTS	MILLIONS
CAVE	MIST
DAREDEVILS	REGION
FALLS	ROUTE
FAME	SEPARATING
FOLKLORE	TIGHTROPE
FORTUNE	UPPER

ANSWER KEY

THE MAIN IDEA

d) The world's most famous waterfall.

UNDERSTANDING WHAT YOU READ

1) Kings and Queens. Presidents and Prime Ministers. Movie stars and artists. Daredevils and thrill-seekers. Newly-married couples and curious sightseers. These are the kinds of people who visit Niagara Falls.
2) Niagara Falls is located nearly half-way down the Niagara River on the international boundary separating New York State and Ontario.
3) Lelawalo was an Indian princess who became known as the "Maid of The Mist." She was set adrift in a canoe and sent over the falls as a sacrifice. According to legend, Lelawalo returned as a spirit, and can still be seen rising through the mists at the bottom of the falls.
4) A school teacher named Annie Edson Taylor was the first person to tumble over the falls in a barrel. She survived the trip in October 24, 1901, but died penniless just 20 years later.

REMEMBERING DETAILS

1) F   Niagara Falls is not even one of the Top 10 highest waterfalls in North America.
2) T
3) F   The word "Niagara" comes from the Indian word "Ohguiaahra" meaning "the Great Thunderer."
4) F   The Great Blondin was a tightrope walker who first crossed the river's giant gorge in 1859.

INFERENCES

1) b
2) d

WORD POWER

1) b
2) b
3) c
4) a
5) b
6) c

FIND-THE-WORDS PUZZLE

H	E	N		U	T	R	O	F	M			F
	O		R	E	P	P	U	I				O
E		R	M		F	A	L	L	S	G		L
P	B	A	R	R	E	L			L	M	N	K
O	F	D	O	O			I	I	A	I		L
R		R	U		R	V		O	J	T		O
T		I	T		E	G		N	O	A		R
H	E	F	E	D			O	S	R	R		E
G	O	T	E					R		A		V
I	N	R	N	O	I	G	E	R	G	P		A
T	A			M	I	S	T			E		C
D	C	A	T	A	R	A	C	T	S	S		

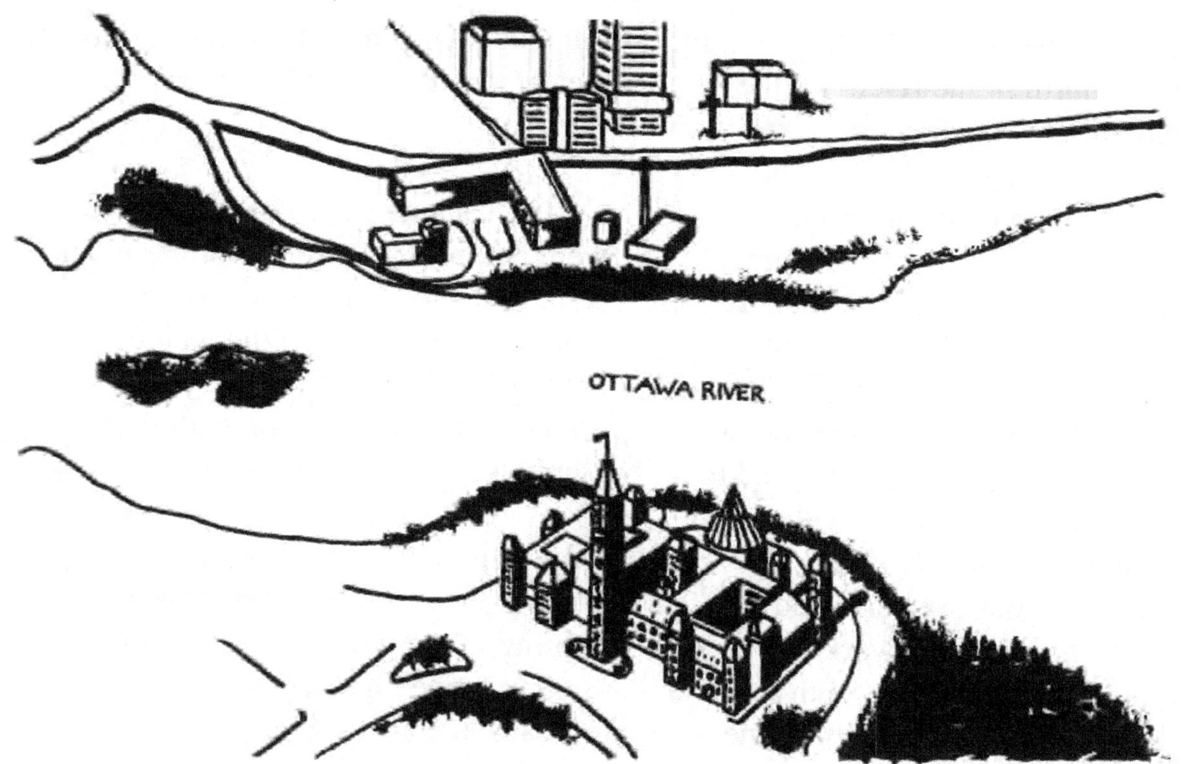

O: Ottawa-Hull

1   In the beginning, they were two backwoods lumber towns built on opposite banks of the fast-flowing Ottawa River. Over a century later, the settlements once known as Wrightstown and Bytown are more than just a part of local history. Together, they form the heart of Canada's Capitol region now called Ottawa-Hull.

2   On the southern shore of the river sits Ottawa, Ontario, the Capital City of Canada. This is where you'll find the Parliament buildings, home to Canada's federal government. Across the river to the north lies Hull, Quebec. The two cities are at the centre of a national capital region which covers 4,662 square kilometres of Western Quebec and Eastern Ontario. Nearly 750,000 French and English-speaking people live in the Ottawa-Hull area, on the border where Canada's two founding European cultures meet.

3   The region has changed a great deal since the days when the Ottawa River was the major travel route of the local Outaouais Indians. The arrival of French explorer Samuel de Champlain in 1613 was the first step in Ottawa-Hull's development. But it was American Philemon Wright who first brought prosperity to the region nearly 200 years later.

4   Wright arrived in 1800 in search of timber to supply to European markets. He bought an area called the Township

of Hull and began to operate a logging business north of the river. As the settlement grew, it became known as Wrightstown, and by 1826 it had a population of a thousand people.

5 This was the same year Colonel John By arrived in Wrightstown from England. Colonel By was hired to supervise the building of the Rideau Canal, a military project designed to connect the Ottawa River with Lake Ontario near Kingston. The construction took six years and involved thousands of workers, many who built houses on the south shore of the river. This settlement opposite Wrightstown soon became known as Bytown.

6 With many sawmills and paper mills attracting more people to the Ottawa Valley, both Bytown and Wrightstown grew into booming lumber towns. On January 1, 1855, Bytown was renamed Ottawa, and exactly three years later England's Queen Victoria chose it as the capital city of the Province of Canada.

7 After Canada's Parliament Buildings were completed in 1865, further plans were made to turn Ottawa into a city worthy of being called the nation's capital. Today, the entire region of Ottawa-Hull is alive with enduring symbols of Canada's history.

8 Visitors to the Rideau Canal can enjoy boating in the summer, and skating in the winter. A trip along Sussex Drive takes you past the home of Canada's Prime Minister. Museums, art galleries, parklands and historic buildings also help attract millions of tourists each year.

9 Best of all, with its mix of French and English culture, Ottawa-Hull stands as a lasting symbol of Canadian unity.

THE MAIN IDEA

Circle the letter of the sentence which best describes the main idea of the article about Ottawa-Hull. Be prepared to support your answer.

a) Canada's National Capital region past and present.
b) Canadian unity on the shores of the Ottawa River.
c) The settling of Wrightstown and Bytown.
d) Two booming lumber towns.

UNDERSTANDING WHAT YOU READ

If you can, answer these questions from memory. If you cannot, look back at the article.

1) What were the original names of Ottawa and Hull?

____

2) How many people live in the Ottawa-Hull area?

____

3) What was Colonel By hired to do?

____

4) Who chose Ottawa as Canada's capital? In what year?

____

REMEMBERING DETAILS

Write TRUE or FALSE under each statement. If the statement is false, write the statement correctly.

1) In the beginning, Ottawa and Hull were backwoods mining towns built on the shores of Lake Ottawa.

____

2) The construction of the Rideau Canal took two years and involved a couple hundred workers.

____

3) A trip along Sussex Drive takes you past museums, galleries and parklands.

____

4) Ottawa-Hull stands as a lasting symbol of Canadian unity.

____ O3

INFERENCES

Based on the article, circle the letter of the best sentence completion.

1) In the beginning in Ottawa-Hull...

a) canoes were the method of transportation of choice.
b) Samuel de Champlain decided it would be a great place for a city.
c) there were enough trees in the area to start a lumber industry.
d) Colonel By and Philemon Wright did not get along.

2) Ottawa and Hull...

a) attracted many settlers because there were jobs there.
b) have always feuded because Queen Victoria chose Ottawa as capital.
c) have too many government workers.
d) would not exist without the Rideau Canal.

INTERPRETATION

1) Go to the library, a tourist information centre or a travel agent and collect as much information as you can about the Ottawa-Hull region.   Plan a trip to Ottawa-Hull. What will you see there? What will you do? Discuss.

2) If you could meet the Prime Minister of Canada, what would you say to him or her? Could you give the Prime Minister any suggestions for improving the country? Discuss.

3) Can you name the capital cities of the ten provinces of Canada? Can you name the capital cities of other countries? Which ones?

WORD POWER

Circle the letter of the word that means the same as the word on the left.

1) founding	a) earliest	b) concrete	c) practical
2) prosperity	a) industry	b) character	c) wealth
3) supervise	a) manage	b) design	c) upset
4) booming	a) rough	b) backward	c) successful
5) worthy	a) cheerless	b) deserving	c) resentful
6) lasting	a) baseless	b) continuing	c) fragmented

FIND-THE-WORDS PUZZLE

You will find words from the article hidden in the box below. Find each word and circle all its letters. To find the words you may have to read from left-to-right, from right-to-left, upward, downward or diagonally. You should be able to find all the words given in the list below the box.

```
S  E  I  R  E  L  L  A  G  X  P  P
D  E  A  L  C  E  N  T  U  R  Y  A
G  S  G  S  M  U  T  I  M  B  E  R
N  D  T  B  U  I  L  T  X  I  S  K
I  O  P  P  O  S  I  T  E  H  K  L
T  O  H  E  L  P  P  R  U  W  F  A
A  W  S  Y  M  B  O  L  S  R  R  N
K  K  A  I  H  S  I  L  G  N  E  D
S  C  X  G  N  I  T  A  O  B  N  S
P  A  R  L  I  A  M  E  N  T  C  H
K  B  M  U  S  E  U  M  S  X  H  C
G  S  T  N  E  M  E  L  T  T  E  S
```

BACKWOODS	MIX
BOATING	MUSEUMS
BUILT	OPPOSITE
CENTURY	PARKLANDS
CULTURES	PARLIAMENT
DEAL	SKATING
ENGLISH	SETTLEMENTS
FRENCH	SIX
GALLERIES	SYMBOLS
HELP	TIMBER

ANSWER KEY

THE MAIN IDEA

a) Canada's National Capital region past and present.

UNDERSTANDING WHAT YOU READ

1) The original names of Ottawa and Hull were Bytown and Wrightstown.
2) Nearly 750,000 French and English-speaking people live in the Ottawa-Hull area.
3) Colonel By was hired to supervise the building of the Rideau Canal, a military project designed to connect the Ottawa River with Lake Ontario near Kingston.
4) England's Queen Victoria chose Ottawa as the capital city of the Province of Canada. She did so in 1858.

REMEMBERING DETAILS

1) F   In the beginning, Ottawa and Hull were two backwoods lumber towns built on opposite banks of the fast-flowing Ottawa River.
2) F   The construction of the Rideau Canal took six years and involved thousands of workers.
3) F   A trip along Sussex Drive takes you past the home of Canada's Prime Minister.
4) T

INFERENCES

1) c
2) a

WORD POWER

1) a
2) c
3) a
4) c
5) b
6) b

FIND-THE-WORDS PUZZLE

```
S  E  I     R  E  L  L  A  G              P
D  E  A  L  C  E  N  T  U  R  Y           A
G  S           U  T  I  M  B  E  R
N  D     B  U  I  L  T  X  I  S  K
I  O  P  P  O  S  I  T  E           L
T  O  H  E  L  P        U        F  A
A  W  S  Y  M  B  O  L  S  R  R  N
K  K     I  H  S  I  L  G  N  E  D
S  C  X  G  N  I  T  A  O  B  N  S
P  A  R  L  I  A  M  E  N  T  C
   B  M  U  S  E  U  M  S        H
   S  T  N  E  M  E  L  T  T  E  S
```

P: The Prairies

1   Ask someone to describe the Canadian Prairies today and you're likely to get a story about waving wheatfields and flat farmland as far as the eye can see. So it comes as quite a shock to discover that Canada's three prairie provinces -- Manitoba, Saskatchewan and Alberta -- were once part of the floor of an ancient sea.

2   It's hard to imagine Canada's prairie heartland sitting at the bottom of a watery sea. But the flat, fertile prairie lands were in fact buried under oceans and glaciers for thousands of years. When the seas had drained and the ice had melted, they left behind the rich soils that today form some of the best farmland in Canada.

3   From the Ontario border in the east to the Rocky Mountain lowlands in the west, Canada's prairie provinces are still very much the flat plains they've always been. But life on the prairies today is far different from the days when the Canadian Pacific Railway first began carrying settlers into Canada's new western frontier.

4   At that time Central Canada was still largely populated by the various tribes of Plains Indians. For centuries, members of the Blackfoot, Blood, Cree, Sioux, Assiniboine, Ojibwa and others had lived on the plains, hunting for buffalo and farming. This was before the western push of immigrants forced many of the Plains Indians off their ancient lands.

5   The push had its beginnings in

Manitoba, Canada's fifth largest province and Ontario's neighbour to the west. The province gets its name from a combination of Sioux and Assiniboine words meaning "prairie water."

6   Before Manitoba was officially recognized as a province in 1870, it had for two hundred years been owned entirely by the Hudson's Bay Company, as were parts of Saskatchewan and Alberta.

7   Manitoba's capital, Winnipeg, is the fourth largest city in Canada with a population of over 600,000 people.

8   Saskatchewan is located between the two prairie provinces of Manitoba and Alberta. It is Canada's sixth largest province. Taking its name from the Indian word meaning "swift flowing," Saskatchewan is often called the "Breadbasket of the World" due to its endless fields of wheat. The provincial capital of Regina was once known as Wascana, an Indian word meaning "pile of bones." The province is also home to cities with such unique Canadian names as Saskatoon and Moose Jaw!

9   Alberta is known more for its rugged wilderness and vast oilfields than for hearty farmlands. Named after the daughter of Queen Victoria, Alberta is home to the famous Leduc oilfields discovered in 1947. The capital city of Edmonton is the northernmost city of its size on the continent, while Calgary was the last Canadian city to host the Winter Olympics. Both Alberta and Saskatchewan became Provinces of Canada in 1905.

10   For three provinces whose history began on the sea bottom, the provinces of Manitoba, Saskatchewan and Alberta have certainly proved they're tops on the prairies!

THE MAIN IDEA

Circle the letter of the sentence which best describes the main idea of the article about the Prairies. Be prepared to support your answer.

a) Former properties of the Hudson's Bay Company.
b) The best wheat in Canada.
c) The result of the push of immigrants.
d) Canada's prairie provinces.

UNDERSTANDING WHAT YOU READ

If you can, answer these questions from memory. If you cannot, look back at the article.

1) What happened when the seas drained off Central Canada?

---

2) Before the Canadian Pacific Railway brought settlers out to the prairies, who lived there?

---

3) What are the names of some cities in Saskatchewan?

---

4) For what is Alberta better known than for its farmland?

REMEMBERING DETAILS

Write TRUE or FALSE under each statement. If the statement is false, write the statement correctly.

1) Ask someone to describe the prairie provinces and you're likely to get a story of coffee bushes and mountainous farmland.

---

2) The word Manitoba means "flat land."

---

3) Saskatchewan is located between New Brunswick and Nova Scotia.

---

4) Both Alberta and Saskatchewan became Provinces of Canada in 1905.

INFERENCES

Based on the article, circle the letter of the best sentence completion.

1) Canadians perceive the prairies as...

a) a gift from the Hudson's Bay Company.
b) not having changed much since the railway was built.
c) ancient seas.
d) wheat farms and flat land.

2) Immigrants to the prairies...

a) immediately recognized the potential for wheat farming on this land.
b) were surprised to see so many buffalo.
c) eventually destroyed the way of life that Plains Indians had enjoyed for generations.
d) came from all over the world.

INTERPRETATION

1) Would you like to be a farmer? Why? Why not? What would you farm? A crop or livestock? What would life be like as a farmer? Discuss.

2) Write a paragraph explaining why you think Regina was once called Wascana, which means pile of bones. Discuss.

3) Life on the prairies today is far different than it was when the Canadian Pacific Railway began bringing settlers to the new western frontier. Was the building of the Canadian Pacific Railway a good thing or a bad thing for Canada?

WORD POWER

Circle the letter of the word that means the same as the word on the left.

1) fertile	a) fruitful	b) barren	c) simple
2) push	a) agony	b) raising	c) thrust
3) swift	a) fast	b) loose	c) free
4) unique	a) funny	b) distinctive	c) elegant
5) hearty	a) steamy	b) caustic	c) mighty
6) tops	a) number one	b) challengers	c) elevated

FIND-THE-WORDS PUZZLE

You will find words from the article hidden in the box below. Find each word and circle all its letters. To find the words you may have to read from left-to-right, from right-to-left, upward, downward or diagonally. You should be able to find all the words given in the list below the box.

```
T  R  I  B  E  S  W  H  E  A  T  D
R  E  I  T  N  O  R  F  H  K  F  R
W  V  P  L  A  I  N  S  F  D  P  A
F  A  D  N  A  L  T  R  A  E  H  I
T  R  V  C  P  S  N  S  R  T  E  N
N  I  H  I  F  L  E  P  M  A  N  E
E  O  L  W  N  I  N  I  L  C  T  D
I  U  V  K  R  G  I  L  A  O  I  E
C  S  P  I  S  L  T  E  N  L  R  I
N  T  A  L  F  V  N  C  D  F  E  R
A  R  H  P  K  C  O  H  S  H  L  U
P  R  O  V  I  N  C  E  S  W  Y  B
```

ANCIENT	PILE
BURIED	PLAINS
CONTINENT	PRAIRIES
DRAINED	PROVINCES
ENTIRELY	SHOCK
FARMLAND	SOILS
FLAT	TRIBES
FRONTIER	VARIOUS
HEARTLAND	WAVING
LOCATED	WHEAT

ANSWER KEY

THE MAIN IDEA

d) Canada's prairie provinces.

UNDERSTANDING WHAT YOU READ

1) When the seas drained off Central Canada, they left behind the rich soils that today form some of the best farmland in Canada.
2) Before the Canadian Pacific Railway brought settlers out to the prairies, Central Canada was still largely populated by the various tribes of Plains Indians. For centuries, members of the Blackfoot, Blood, Cree, Sioux, Assiniboine, Ojibwa and others had lived on the plains, hunting for buffalo and farming.
3) Names of cities in Saskatchewan include Saskatoon, Regina and Moose Jaw.
4) Alberta is better known for its rugged wilderness and vast oilfields than for its farmlands.

REMEMBERING DETAILS

1) F   Ask someone to describe the Canadian Prairies today and you're likely to get a story about waving wheatfields and flat farmland as far as the eye can see.
2) F   The word Manitoba means "prairie water."
3) F   Saskatchewan is located between Manitoba and Alberta.
4) T

INFERENCES

1) d
2) c

WORD POWER

1) a
2) c
3) a
4) h
5) c
6) a

FIND-THE-WORDS PUZZLE

```
T R I B E S W H E A T D
R E I T N O R F       R
W V P L A I N S F D    A
  A D N A L T R A E H I
T R V     S N S R T E N
N I   I     E P M A N E
E O     N I N I L C T D
I U     R G I L A O I E
C S   I     T E N L R I
N T A L F   N   D   E R
A R     K C O H S   L U
P R O V I N C E S   Y B
```

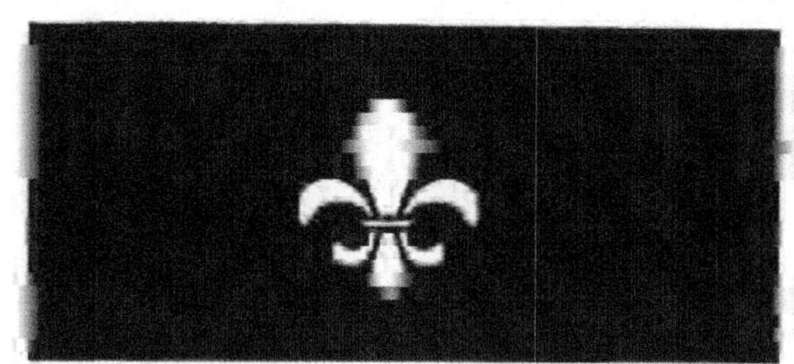 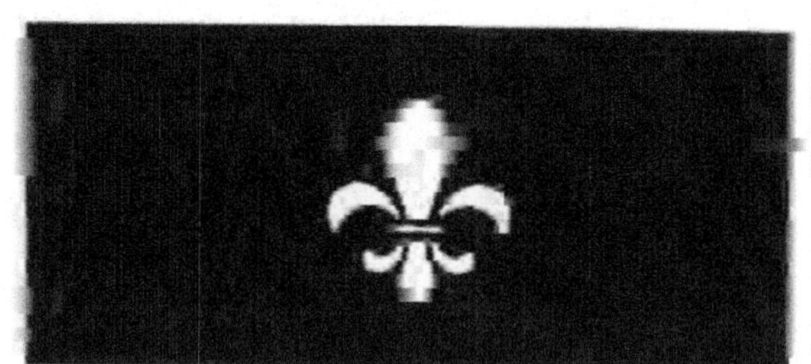

Q: Quebec

1 In the course of history, it has been known as both New France and Lower Canada. To the Algonkian Indians, it was called *kebec*, meaning "the place where the river narrows." Today, the province that grew up along a narrow stretch of the mighty St. Lawrence River is known proudly as Quebec.

2 As Canada's largest and most distinct province, Quebec has played a very important role in Canadian history since the time of its discovery by Europeans in 1534. This was the year that famed French explorer Jacques Cartier landed on the tip of Quebec's Gaspe Peninsula and claimed the land for the King of France.

3 The following year, Cartier returned and sailed inland past the Indian village of Stradacona (now Quebec City) and up the St. Lawrence River to Hochelaga (now Montreal). His voyage marked the beginning of what was to become New France.

4 In 1608, explorer Samuel de Champlain arrived from France to build a trading post at the site of Quebec City and establish French colonies in the area. By 1663, Quebec City had grown to become the official capital city of the Royal Province of New France and a major centre for the fur trade in North America.

5 The struggle to protect the new French colonies and their investment in the fur trade led France into an

ongoing war with Britain for control of Quebec and surrounding areas. This ended in 1763, when Britain defeated France on the Plains of Abraham and New France was awarded to England.

6   However, the Quebec Act of 1774 guaranteed the conquered French settlers the right to maintain their French language, religion and institutions while living under English rule.

7   Although the Act was meant to bring French and English together, the co-existence of two cultures with such a history of conflict has caused ongoing problems for Canadian national unity. Although Quebec is united with the rest of Canada by history and geography, it is separated by both French language and culture. With the last major immigration from France occurring before 1670, the ancestors of nearly all today's French-Canadians have roots in Quebec dating back nearly 300 years. This is one reason why many Quebecers speak of their province with such fierce pride.

These tensions haven't kept Quebec   8 from becoming a popular destination for tourists. Travellers to old Quebec City can see original buildings dating back to the 1600s. In Montreal, sports fans can watch the world's most famous hockey team, the Canadiens, or enjoy an afternoon watching the Expos play baseball in beautiful Olympic Stadium.

Hundreds of miles north of Quebec's 9 urban areas lies the rugged Quebec wilderness, a remote land of rocky plains, dense forests and endless rivers. Other than the Native people who call it home, few Quebecers have ever visited the vast northern regions of this huge province.

There's no guarantee that Quebec   10 will remain a part of Canada in the future. However, there is no question that La Belle Province has played a major role in Canada's past.

THE MAIN IDEA

Circle the letter of the sentence which best describes the main idea of the article about Quebec. Be prepared to support your answer.

a) The national unity question.
b) The province of Quebec.
c) Canada's future neighbour.
d) French colonies in Canada.

UNDERSTANDING WHAT YOU READ

If you can, answer these questions from memory. If you cannot, look back at the article.

1) What does the word Quebec mean?

____

2) What did Champlain do in 1608?

____

3) What did the Quebec Act of 1774 guarantee?

____

4) What are Quebec's northern regions like?

____

REMEMBERING DETAILS

Write TRUE or FALSE under each statement. If the statement is false, write the statement correctly.

1) Quebec has played a very important role in Canadian history since the time of its discovery in 1534.

____

2) The French wanted to protect the new French colonies from the British to secure their interests in the maple syrup industry.

____

3) All the French-speaking people in Quebec today are recent immigrants.

____

4) Quebec will surely remain a part of Canada forever.

____

INFERENCES

Based on the article, circle the letter of the best sentence completion.

1) There is the possibility that...

a) the Quebec Act of 1774 will be rewritten.
b) Quebec will change its name.
c) France and Britain will once again go to war over Quebec.
d) Quebec will one day leave the Canadian Confederation.

2) The Quebec Act of 1774...

a) failed to do what it was designed to do.
b) worked for the first 200 years.
c) was changed by an act of Parliament in 1976.
d) was never agreed to by the French.

INTERPRETATION

1) Canadian unity has been an issue for many years. For the next while check
   available newspapers for articles dealing with the issue of Canadian unity. Cut
   these articles out and bring them to class. Discuss the issue.

2) Canadian unity has been an issue for many years. Organize the class into
   groups representing the Quebec side of the issue and the Canadian side of the
   issue. As a class hold a constitutional debate.

3) Write a letter to the Premier of Quebec detailing reasons why you think
   Quebec should stay in Canada. Or, write a letter to the Prime Minister of
   Canada detailing reasons why you think Quebec should become a sovereign
   nation.

WORD POWER

Circle the letter of the word that means the same as the word on the left.

1) course	a) lane	b) progression	c) safari
2) distinct	a) different	b) flattered	c) radiant
3) struggle	a) annoyance	b) problem	c) effort
4) awarded	a) fastened	b) given	c) prized
5) rule	a) regret	b) administration	c) borders
6) dense	a) thick	b) leafy	c) tropical

FIND-THE-WORDS PUZZLE

You will find words from the article hidden in the box below. Find each word and circle all its letters. To find the words you may have to read from left-to-right, from right-to-left, upward, downward or diagonally. You should be able to find all the words given in the list below the box.

```
R  U  G  G  E  D  R  N  N  S  V  C
R  O  L  E  D  E  M  A  F  M  O  O
C  F  P  A  B  E  H  B  E  N  Y  N
H  F  A  C  T  T  O  R  Q  G  A  G
Y  I  C  N  W  N  H  U  O  Y  G  O
S  C  W  Q  S  A  E  U  T  Y  E  I
W  I  G  K  T  R  G  I  G  O  S  N
O  A  N  S  E  A  N  L  H  E  P  G
R  L  O  D  L  U  F  I  E  R  C  E
R  P  L  A  N  G  U  A  G  E  W  F
A  P  L  A  C  E  R  U  T  L  U  C
N  I  A  T  N  I  A  M  Q  N  O  C
```

ACT	NARROWS
CONQUERED	OFFICIAL
CULTURE	ONGOING
FAMED	PLACE
FANS	POST
FIERCE	ROLE
GUARANTEED	RUGGED
HUGE	UNITY
LANGUAGE	URBAN
MAINTAIN	VOYAGES

ANSWER KEY

THE MAIN IDEA

b) The province of Quebec.

UNDERSTANDING WHAT YOU READ

1) The word Quebec means the place where the river narrows.
2) In 1608, explorer Samuel de Champlain arrived from France to build a trading post at the site of Quebec City and establish French colonies in the area.
3) The Quebec Act of 1774 guaranteed the conquered French settlers the right to maintain their French language, religion and institutions while living under English rule.
4) Quebec's northern regions are a remote land of both rocky plains, dense forests and endless rivers.

REMEMBERING DETAILS

1) T
2) F   The French wanted to protect the new French colonies from the British to secure their interests in the fur trade.
3) F   With the last major immigration from France occurring before 1670, the ancestors of nearly all today's French-Canadians have roots in Quebec dating back nearly 300 years.
4) F   There's no guarantee that Quebec will remain a part of Canada in the future.

INFERENCES

1) d
2) a

WORD POWER

1) b
2) a
3) c
4) b
5) b
6) a

FIND-THE-WORDS PUZZLE

R	U	G	G	E	D		N			V		C
R	O	L	E	D	E	M	A	F		O		O
	F				E		B		N	Y		N
	F	A	C	T	T		R	Q		A		G
	I		N		N	H	U		Y	G		O
S	C			S	A	E	U	T		E		I
W	I			T	R		I	G		S		N
O	A		S	E	A	N			E			G
R	L	O	D		U	F	I		E	R	C	E
R	P	L	A	N	G	U	A	G	E			
A	P	L	A	C	E	R	U	T	L	U	C	
N	I	A	T	N	I	A	M					

R: Rupert's Land

1   In terms of total land mass, Canada's 10 provinces and two territories help make it the second largest country in the world. But up until 1870, forty percent of what is now Canada was known to explorers and fur traders by a different name, RUPERT'S LAND.

2   The story of Canada's growth as a country cannot be told without tracing the history of Rupert's Land, for this vast wilderness area was at the heart of the rich fur trade on which Canada was built. Much of the credit for exploring and developing this area goes to the fur-trading adventurers of the Hudson's Bay Company, which held total control over all of Rupert's Land for 200 years beginning in 1670.

3   That was the year a group of British businessmen convinced King Charles II of England to give them a large portion of unexplored land in North America. Their hope was to tap into the beaver-rich areas between Lake Superior and Hudson Bay by fur-trading with local Indians.

4   A charter from the King granted the founders of the newly-formed Hudson's Bay Company sole rights to trade on the land. He also awarded company founders the title of "Lords of the land forever." This gave the Hudson's Bay Company the right to govern all fur-trading activities conducted in Rupert's Land.

5   In return for this generous donation to the company, all the King requested was a gift of two elks and two black

beavers each time his heirs and future Kings travelled to the land. However, had the King known the actual size of the gift he was giving, he might have asked for more in return, for it amounted to an area almost forty percent of the size of Canada today.

6   Named in honour of Prince Rupert, who was a cousin to the King, Rupert's Land included much of northern Quebec and Ontario, the entire Province of Manitoba, a great deal of southern Saskatchewan and Alberta, the eastern part of the Northwest Territories, and parts of Minnesota and North Dakota south of the border. The area was so rich in furs that within 10 years the Hudson's Bay Company had fur-trading posts on all the major rivers running through Rupert's Land.

7   When the Hudson's Bay Company was given title to the land by the British, French fur-trappers felt the company was becoming a threat to the French fur trade. In 1686, a French military force raided and captured many of the company's fur-trading posts. This was the primary reason Britain gave for declaring war with France from 1689 to 1713.

8   When the war was over, most of the posts were returned to the Hudson's Bay Company, but competition in the area continued. In 1783, the Northwest Company began trapping in the area, and soon became a bitter rival of the Hudson's Bay Company. That ended in 1821 with the merger of the two companies.

9   By the 1860s, the Canadian government was under pressure to regain control of Rupert's Land and make it part of Canada. On July 15, 1870, Rupert's Land was purchased from the Hudson's Bay Company for 300,000 English pounds, and the next phase in Canada's development was under way.

THE MAIN IDEA

Circle the letter of the sentence which best describes the main idea of the article about Rupert's Land. Be prepared to support your answer.

a) The Hudson's Bay Company.
b) Rupert's Land.
c) The enormous size of Rupert's Land.
d) The King's generous donation.

UNDERSTANDING WHAT YOU READ

If you can, answer these questions from memory. If you cannot, look back at the article.

1) What did a group of British businessmen convince King Charles II to do? In having the King do this, what was their hope?

____

2) What did the King ask for in return for his donation?

____

3) What land did Rupert's Land include?

____

4) How did the feud between the Hudson's Bay Company and the Northwest Company end?

____

REMEMBERING DETAILS

Write TRUE or FALSE under each statement. If the statement is false, write the statement correctly.

1) The Hudson's Bay Company was never in control of Rupert's Land.

____

2) Had the King known the actual size of his gift, he might have asked for more in return.

____

3) After being given Rupert's Land by the King, the businessmen were disappointed to find there were barely any furs to be traded.

____

4) French fur-trappers did not mind that the English were given title to the land by the British, and were trapping furs on the same territory as the French.

____

INFERENCES

Based on the article, circle the letter of the best sentence completion.

1) The English and French...

a) eventually split Rupert's Land down the middle.
b) still hold a grudge over the fur trade.
c) thought fur was a good enough reason to go to war with each other.
d) both helped wipe out the fur trade.

2) The success of the Hudson's Bay Company...

a) shows that at one time there was an abundance of wild animals in Canada.
b) proves the owners were shrewd businessmen.
c) is the example upon which many modern day companies model themselves.
d) was just pure luck.

INTERPRETATION

1) It can be said that Canada was built upon the backs of furbearers, animals with fur. What is meant by this? Why were furs so important in Europe? Discuss.

2) Write a short composition about the chance meeting in the woods of an English fur-trapper and a French fur-trapper. What would they say to each other?

3) Even today, some hunting is done for wild animals to be sold for their various parts. Name some of these animals and the parts they are hunted for. What will these parts be used for? Can this hunting be stopped? Should it be? Discuss.

WORD POWER

Circle the letter of the word that means the same as the word on the left.

1) tracing	a) dramatizing	b) reverberating	c) outlining
2) portion	a) ravine	b) pie	c) piece
3) donation	a) gift	b) slight	c) invoice
4) heirs	a) followers	b) offspring	c) organization
5) merger	a) joining	b) disbanding	c) segregation
6) under way	a) slowed down	b) caught up	c) in motion

FIND-THE-WORDS PUZZLE

You will find words from the article hidden in the box below. Find each word and circle all its letters. To find the words you may have to read from left-to-right, from right-to-left, upward, downward or diagonally. You should be able to find all the words given in the list below the box.

C	O	M	P	E	T	I	T	I	O	N	D
H	O	P	E	E	L	O	S	L	A	V	E
O	B	N	R	A	I	D	E	D	D	H	T
P	I	I	D	T	A	P	L	E	V	B	N
W	T	A	K	U	P	H	T	S	E	S	U
S	T	G	C	U	C	G	I	A	N	R	O
S	E	E	T	M	N	T	T	H	T	E	M
A	R	R	G	I	I	M	E	P	U	D	A
M	E	O	N	D	S	H	P	D	R	A	R
G	E	N	E	R	O	U	S	L	E	R	D
V	U	R	A	S	L	A	V	I	R	T	A
R	C	O	U	S	I	N	F	T	S	A	V

ADVENTURERS	PHASE
AMOUNTED	RAIDED
BITTER	REGAIN
COMPETITION	RIVALS
CONDUCTED	RUNNING
COUSIN	SOLE
CREDIT	TAP
GENEROUS	TITLE
HOPE	TRADERS
MASS	VAST

ANSWER KEY

THE MAIN IDEA

b) Rupert's Land.

UNDERSTANDING WHAT YOU READ

1) A group of British businessmen convinced King Charles II of England to give them a large portion of unexplored land in North America. Their hope was to tap into the beaver-rich areas between Lake Superior and Hudson Bay by fur-trading with local Indians.
2) In return for this generous donation to the company, all the King requested was a gift of two elks and two black beavers each time his heirs and future Kings travelled to the land.
3) Rupert's Land included much of northern Quebec and Ontario, the entire Province of Manitoba, a great deal of southern Saskatchewan and Alberta, the eastern part of the Northwest Territories, and parts of Minnesota and North Dakota south of the border.
4) The feud between the Hudson's Bay Company and the Northwest Company ended in 1821 with the merger of the two companies.

REMEMBERING DETAILS

1) F   The Hudson's Bay Company held total control over all of Rupert's Land for 200 years beginning in 1670.
2) T
3) F   The area was so rich in furs that within 10 years the Hudson's Bay Company had fur-trading posts on all the major rivers running through Rupert's Land.
4) F   French fur-trappers felt the English were becoming a threat to the French fur trade. In 1686, a French military force raided and captured many of the Hudson's Bay Company's fur-trading posts.

INFERENCES

1) c
2) a

WORD POWER

1) c
2) c
3) a
4) b
5) a
6) c

FIND-THE-WORDS PUZZLE

```
C O M P E T I T I O N D
H O P E E L O S   A   E
  B N R A I D E D D   T
  I I D T A P L E V   N
  T A   U     T S E   U
S T G   C G   I A N R O
S E E   N   T T H T E M
A R R   I I E E P U D A
M     N D       D R A
G E N E R O U S   E R
  U R   S L A V I R T
R C O U S I N V T S A V
```

S: Skydome

1   "The sky's the limit" is a saying used by people who believe anything is possible if you dare to dream big. In Toronto, it took some mighty big dreamers to come up with the idea for the world's most remarkable domed stadium, SkyDome.

2   SkyDome isn't the world's first domed stadium. That honour goes to the Astrodome, a stadium built by the City of Houston, Texas in 1964. But SkyDome is the only stadium with a roof that can open and close, making it the first fully "retractable" roof in the world. With three of its four giant roof panels able to move, SkyDome can change from a closed dome to an open-air stadium in just 20 minutes.

3   The idea to build a domed stadium in Toronto was first suggested by a group of investors in 1983. Over 34 possible locations across the city were carefully considered. Eventually, it was decided that "the Dome" would be built on old Canadian National Railway lands beside the CN Tower, close to Toronto's waterfront on the northern shores of Lake Ontario.

4   In 1985, a stadium design was selected; it included plans for the retractable roof. The cost to complete the project was originally estimated to be $184 million. Construction officially began on October 3, 1986, and was expected to last 32 months.

5   By the time it was finished in 1989, the cost to build SkyDome had risen to nearly $600 million. Many people

were outraged by the cost, feeling this was far too much money to spend on a sports stadium. But facts about the construction seemed to suggest the money was well spent.

6   For example, during SkyDome's construction, workers used enough concrete to pour a sidewalk from Toronto to Montreal. The roof alone weighs in at 11,000 tons, an amount equal to the weight of 3,732 automobiles. It covers a total of eight acres and spans 209 metres across at its widest point.

7   At its highest point, the SkyDome rises 86 metres. It can fit a 31 storey building inside with the roof closed. On the ground, a total of 743 Indian elephants, or 8 Boeing 747 jumbo-jets, can fit comfortably on the playing field. Nearly 193 kilometres of cable handle the power needs at SkyDome, which requires enough electricity to light an entire city.

8   Other special features include the JumboTron, one of the largest video screens in the world. The JumboTron is three storeys high and cost $17 million. SkyDome is also home to a 348-room hotel, a fitness club, a theatre, seven restaurants, and the largest MacDonald's in North America.

9   Since opening on June 3, 1989, over 30 million people have visited SkyDome, making it Toronto's most popular attraction. Events at the Dome have included everything from concerts to motorcycle racing, but by far the biggest attraction has been Toronto's professional baseball team, the Blue Jays. In 1992, the Jays won their first World Series championship and attracted over 4 million people to SkyDome that baseball season!

10   With a one-of-a-kind roof and many attractions, it's no wonder SkyDome is called "the world's greatest entertainment centre."

THE MAIN IDEA

Circle the letter of the sentence which best describes the main idea of the article about SkyDome. Be prepared to support your answer.

a) The world's greatest entertainment centre.
b) Attractions coming to SkyDome.
c) The world's first fully retractable roof.
d) The costs involved in building a sports stadium.

UNDERSTANDING WHAT YOU READ

If you can, answer these questions from memory. If you cannot, look back at the article.

1) Who first suggested building a domed stadium in Toronto? When?

2) Where was SkyDome built?

3) How many elephants or jumbo-jets could fit in SkyDome?

4) What kinds of events are held at SkyDome?

REMEMBERING DETAILS

Write TRUE or FALSE under each statement. If the statement is false, write the statement correctly.

1) SkyDome is the world's first domed stadium.

2) Building SkyDome was supposed to cost $184 million, but ended up costing nearly $600 million.

3) Enough concrete was used in building SkyDome to pour a sidewalk from Winnipeg to Vancouver.

4) In 1992, the Blue Jays had the worst team in baseball and only 350,000 fans attended their games.

INFERENCES

Based on the article, circle the letter of the best sentence completion.

1) The people who decided to build SkyDome...

a) knew the Blue Jays would win the World Series in 1992.
b) underestimated terribly how much construction would cost.
c) were worried the roof would not work.
d) eat at MacDonald's often.

2) The people who were outraged about the cost to build SkyDome...

a) no longer thought it was too much to spend on a stadium when it was finished.
b) do not like the Blue Jays.
c) refuse to go to SkyDome.
d) thought it would have been better to spend the money on other things.

INTERPRETATION

1) Have you ever been to SkyDome? What did you see there? What other
   stadiums have you been in? Where? What did you see there? Discuss.

2) Write a short composition and call it: The Night I Appeared At SkyDome.
   Share your story with the class.

3) Why do you think the cost of building SkyDome rose so dramatically?
   Should so much money be spent on a stadium? Or should that money be used
   for other things? Like what? Discuss.

WORD POWER

Circle the letter of the word that means the same as the word on the left.

1) dare	a) contrive	b) risk	c) swear
2) suggested	a) nominated	b) proposed	c) foretold
3) outraged	a) horrified	b) modified	c) settled
4) spans	a) extends	b) climbs	c) wavers
5) handle	a) multiply	b) frazzle	c) control
6) attractions	a) investments	b) innings	c) shows

FIND-THE-WORDS PUZZLE

You will find words from the article hidden in the box below. Find each word and circle all its letters. To find the words you may have to read from left-to-right, from right-to-left, upward, downward or diagonally. You should be able to find all the words given in the list below the box.

```
S   I   D   E   W   A   L   K   C   B   F   P
T   N   O   R   F   R   E   T   A   W   I   T
R   V   R   A   C   I   N   G   T   H   C   H
E   E   L   B   A   C   E   D   S   V   O   E
C   S   L   I   S   W   M   N   C   M   N   A
N   T   A   D   E   M   O   D   R   U   C   T
O   O   B   E   G   I   D   T   E   I   R   R
C   R   E   A   P   F   Y   O   E   D   E   E
I   S   S   M   M   B   K   N   N   A   T   R
T   V   A   C   R   E   S   S   S   T   E   C
Y   H   B   F   I   T   N   E   S   S   W   P
C   R   E   T   R   A   C   T   A   B   L   E
```

ACRES	INVESTORS
BASEBALL	RACING
CABLE	RETRACTABLE
CHAMPIONSHIP	SCREENS
CITY	SIDEWALK
CONCERTS	SKYDOME
CONCRETE	STADIUM
DOMED	THEATRE
FITNESS	TONS
IDEA	WATERFRONT

ANSWER KEY

THE MAIN IDEA

a) The world's greatest entertainment centre.

UNDERSTANDING WHAT YOU READ

1) The idea to build a domed stadium in Toronto was first suggested by a group of investors in 1983.
2) Skydome was built on old Canadian National Railway lands beside the CN Tower, close to Toronto's waterfront on the northern shores of Lake Ontario.
3) A total of 743 Indian elephants, or 8 Boeing 747 jumbo-jets, can fit comfortably on the playing field of SkyDome.
4) Events at the Dome have included everything from concerts to motorcycle racing, but by far the biggest attraction has been Toronto's professional baseball team, the Blue Jays.

REMEMBERING DETAILS

1) F SkyDome isn't the world's first domed stadium. That honour goes to the Astrodome, a stadium built by the City of Houston, Texas in 1964.
2) T
3) F Enough concrete was used in building SkyDome to pour a sidewalk from Toronto to Montreal.
4) F In 1992, the Blue Jays won their first World Series championship and attracted over 4 million people to SkyDome that baseball season!

INFERENCES

1) b
2) d

WORD POWER

1) b
2) b
3) a
4) a
5) c
6) c

FIND-THE-WORDS PUZZLE

S	I	D	E	W	A	L	K				P
T	N	O	R	F	R	E	T	A	W	I	T
R	V	R	A	C	I	N	G		H	C	H
E	E	L	B	A	C	E		S		O	E
C	S	L	I			M	N	C	M	N	A
N	T	A	D	E	M	O	D	R	U	C	T
O	O	B	E		I	D	T	E	I	R	R
C	R	E	A	P		Y	O	E	D	E	E
I	S	S	M			K	N	N	A	T	
T		A	C	R	E	S	S	S	T	E	
Y	H	B	F	I	T	N	E	S	S		
C	R	E	T	R	A	C	T	A	B	L	E

T: Trans Canada Highway

1   When Europeans first arrived here, they explored Eastern Canada by travelling across its waters. Later, the steel tracks of the railroad linked east and west. Today motorists can travel from coast to coast on a ribbon of asphalt and concrete called the Trans Canada Highway.

2   From St. John's, Newfoundland in the east to Victoria, British Columbia in the west, the Trans Canada Highway begins and ends on an island. In between it runs coast to coast through Canada's 10 provinces, stretching nearly 7,780 kilometres across the entire country.

3   Heading west from the Atlantic coast, motorists on the Trans Canada travel by ferry to the mainland, through the Maritime Provinces, past the historic cities of Montreal and Quebec and across Ontario to the northern shores of the Great Lakes Huron and Superior. Driving beyond Manitoba to the Prairies, the Trans Canada runs straight and smooth, as it cuts through vast fields of wheat and towering oil fields. Then comes the long climb up Rogers Pass over the Rocky Mountains, through the deep valleys and on towards the coast. With a quick ferry ride to Vancouver Island, the highway ends at Victoria.

4   Unlike this super-highway, the first roads in Canada were little more than Indian trails. They were used to connect rivers and lakes, or to travel

around rapids too dangerous for canoes. In a culture without the wheel, the canoe was the main method of travel for most Indians. When the French and British began settling in Canada, they discovered a country unsuitable for European-style roadways. Thick uncut forests, endless waterways, hills and mountains provided major obstacles for building easy travel routes.

5 Once the first automobiles arrived in Canada, however, the idea for a coast-to-coast highway quickly followed. In 1910, a group of motorists formed the Canadian Highway Association. Their dream of a national highway helped get both federal and provincial governments working together to build better road systems across the country.

6 In 1949, the Parliament of Canada passed the Trans Canada Highway Act. It called for the construction of a hard-surfaced, all-weather road from coast to coast. The highway was to be completed by 1956 at a cost of $300 million.

7 When work began the following summer, it proved to be more difficult and expensive than anyone imagined. Workmen often had to blast through hundreds of metres of solid rock. In Glacier National Park in British Columbia, snow sheds had to be built to protect workers from avalanches. In all, 25 major bridges had to be built over rivers and rugged land. These delays helped drive the cost of construction to over $1 billion.

8 When tunnels through the mountains of British Columbia were finished, the highway was considered complete. On July 30th, 1962, in a ceremony conducted at Rogers Pass, the longest national highway in the world was officially opened to the public. Since that time, the Trans Canada Highway has brought Canadians together from coast to coast.

THE MAIN IDEA

Circle the letter of the sentence which best describes the main idea of the article about the Trans Canada Highway. Be prepared to support your answer.

a) Different ways to travel across Canada.
b) The passing of the Trans Canada Highway Act.
c) The road that connects Canada from east to west.
d) The difficulty Canada's terrain presents for road construction.

UNDERSTANDING WHAT YOU READ

If you can, answer these questions from memory. If you cannot, look back at the article.

1) What were the first roads in Canada like? What were they used for?

____

2) What did the Canadian Highway Association help do?

____

3) Why did the early settlers in Canada not build European-style roadways?

____

4) What caused the building of the highway to take longer than expected?

____

REMEMBERING DETAILS

Write TRUE or FALSE under each statement. If the statement is false, write the statement correctly.

1) The Trans Canada Highway runs through six provinces and stretches nearly 5,000 kilometres.

____

2) After automobiles arrived in Canada, it took a long time for someone to get the idea to build a highway from coast to coast.

____

3) The Trans Canada Highway Act called for the building of a hard-surfaced, all-weather road from coast to coast.

____

4) There was no danger involved in constructing the Trans Canada Highway.

____

INFERENCES

Based on the article, circle the letter of the best sentence completion.

1) The Trans Canada Highway...

a) was built to ensure that the automobile industry would survive in Canada.
b) has made it easier for Canadians to travel.
c) is dangerous during winter months.
d) would not exist without the ferry boats to Newfoundland and Vancouver Island.

2) When the Trans Canada Highway was built...

a) the many obstacles presented by Mother Nature had to be overcome.
b) gasoline was much cheaper to buy.
c) the country nearly went broke because the highway cost so much.
d) many workmen quit because the job was too difficult.

INTERPRETATION

1) What would the world be like if the wheel had never been invented? Write a
   short composition describing what life would be like. Discuss.

2) How will we travel in the future? How will any newly invented modes of
   transport affect Canada, Canadians and the world? Discuss.

3) Using a map of Canada, trace the Trans Canada Highway from coast to coast.
   Write down the names of large cities and lakes and rivers you would pass
   travelling across the country.

WORD POWER

Circle the letter of the word that means the same as the word on the left.

1) linked	a) depended	b) joined	c) offered
2) beyond	a) before	b) on top of	c) farther than
3) method	a) manner	b) sport	c) help
4) unsuitable	a) unaccustomed	b) unfit	c) unskilled
5) sheds	a) beams	b) plows	c) shelters
6) conducted	a) held	b) guided	c) operated

FIND-THE-WORDS PUZZLE

You will find words from the article hidden in the box below. Find each word and circle all its letters. To find the words you may have to read from left-to-right, from right-to-left, upward, downward or diagonally. You should be able to find all the words given in the list below the box.

H	I	S	T	O	R	I	C	L	Y	T	B
H	P	R	H	T	A	E	Y	S	A	A	A
V	U	E	I	O	I	L	T	N	W	E	I
S	B	M	C	M	L	R	S	O	H	H	R
L	L	M	K	W	R	I	A	W	G	W	O
S	I	U	L	M	O	T	O	R	I	S	T
Y	C	S	Z	Q	A	E	C	O	H	H	C
E	M	A	E	R	D	R	T	U	E	O	I
L	D	N	N	K	H	I	L	T	L	R	V
L	L	L	C	O	S	T	J	E	G	E	S
A	D	O	A	F	E	N	L	S	T	S	E
V	R	D	A	N	G	E	R	O	U	S	Y

CANOE	RAILROAD
COAST	ROCK
DANGEROUS	ROUTES
DREAM	SHORES
ENTIRE	SNOW
HIGHWAY	SUMMER
HISTORIC	THICK
MOTORIST	VALLEYS
OIL	VICTORIA
PUBLIC	WHEAT

ANSWER KEY

THE MAIN IDEA

b) The road that connects Canada from east to west.

UNDERSTANDING WHAT YOU READ

1) The first roads in Canada were nothing more than Indian trails. These roads were used to connect rivers and lakes, or to travel around rapids too dangerous for canoes.
2) The Canadian Highway Association helped get both the federal and provincial governments to work together to build better road systems across Canada.
3) Early settlers did not build European-style roadways because thick uncut forests, endless waterways, hills and mountains provided major obstacles for building easy travel routes.
4) Building the Trans Canada Highway took longer than expected because the job proved to be more difficult and expensive than anyone imagined.

REMEMBERING DETAILS

1) F   The Trans Canada Highway runs through all ten provinces and stretches nearly 7,780 kilometres.
2) F   Once the first automobiles arrived in Canada, the idea for a coast-to-coast highway quickly followed.
3) T
4) F   There was a lot of danger involved in building the Trans Canada Highway. Workmen often had to blast through hundreds of metres of solid rock. They had to build 25 bridges over rivers and rugged land and they faced the danger of avalanches in Glacier National Park.

INFERENCES

1) b
2) a

WORD POWER

1) b
2) c
3) a
4) b
5) c
6) a

FIND-THE-WORDS PUZZLE

H	I	S	T	O	R	I	C		Y	T	
	P	R	H		A			S	A	A	A
	U	E	I	O	I	L	T	N	W	E	I
	B	M	C		L		S	O	H	H	R
	L	M	K		R		A	W	G	W	O
S	I	U		M	O	T	O	R	I	S	T
Y	C	S			A	E	C	O	H	H	C
E	M	A	E	R	D	R		U		O	I
L			N	K		I		T		R	V
L			C	O		T		E		E	
A		Q			E	N		S		S	
V	R	D	A	N	G	E	R	O	U	S	

Josiah Henson 1789-1883

U: Uncle Tom's Cabin

1 Uncle Tom's Cabin is considered an important symbol of the arrival of early Black immigrants to Canada. It is also considered a lasting reminder of the ongoing struggle for social equality facing many Blacks in North America today. In either case, there is no denying Uncle Tom's Cabin its place in Canadian history.

2 The tiny cabin located in Dresden, Ontario takes its name from the title of a famous novel that was written in 1852 by American author Harriot Beecher Stowe. The building is recognized for the fact it was once home to a former slave whose life story helped inspire Miss Stowe to write her book.

3 That man was Josiah Henson, who was born June 15, 1789 and wound up a slave in the southern United States. In 1830 he decided to flee to Canada, which had already passed an antislavery law in 1793. Henson was part of the first wave of Black immigrants into Canada. Most of these new Canadians were escaping slaves who believed that crossing the border meant safety and freedom.

4 It is estimated that as many as fifty-thousand Blacks may have entered Canada in the first half of the 1800s. Fortunately, Henson was an intelligent man and a preacher who adjusted quickly to a life of freedom in Canada. However, he grew concerned about the living conditions of many of the Black fugitives entering Canada. He soon began devoting much of his time to the

problem of how they might best adjust to their new life.

5   In 1840, Henson was part of a Southwestern Ontario group that founded the British-American Institute, a trade school for Blacks that offered instruction in such skills as carpentry, smithery, cooking and sewing. To help raise money for the school, Henson decided to publish his life story, called "The Life of Josiah Henson, Formerly A Slave, Now an Inhabitant of Canada."

6   Three years after its publication, the story came to the attention of Harriet Stowe. She was already working on a book about the evils of slavery, but Henson's story inspired her to finish it. Stowe's novel, "Uncle Tom's Cabin," was an instant success, selling 5,000 copies across the northern U.S., Canada and Britain in one week.

7   The book detailed the sad life of a faithful Black slave. Although Stowe never admitted publicly that Henson was the model for Uncle Tom, his link to the story was so strong he soon became a celebrity. He lectured, travelled and met Queen Victoria. He also became an anti-slavery activist and an early leader in Canada's Black community.

8   After his death in 1883, Henson's cabin and grave became tourist attractions. Dresden began advertising itself as "The Home of Uncle Tom," and in 1948 the cabin was turned into a museum.

9   The name "Uncle Tom" soon took on a negative meaning far different from the character of the man who inspired it. But the name Josiah Henson still stands as a positive reminder of the new life early Black settlers found upon arriving in Canada.

THE MAIN IDEA

Circle the letter of the sentence which best describes the main idea of the article about Uncle Tom's Cabin. Be prepared to support your answer.

a) Harriet Beecher Stowe's "Uncle Tom's Cabin".
b) The life in Canada of a former slave.
c) The museum in Dresden, Ontario.
d) The man who inspired the novel "Uncle Tom's Cabin".

UNDERSTANDING WHAT YOU READ

If you can, answer these questions from memory. If you cannot, look back at the article.

1) Why is the tiny cabin in Dresden famous?

---

2) How many Black people came to Canada in the early 1800s? Why did they come?

---

3) What was the British-American Institute?

---

4) What is the novel "Uncle Tom's Cabin" about?

REMEMBERING DETAILS

Write TRUE or FALSE under each statement. If the statement is false, write the statement correctly.

1) Josiah Henson was an intelligent man and a preacher who adjusted quickly to a life of freedom in Canada.

---

2) In an attempt to get rich, Josiah Henson published his life story.

---

3) People remember Josiah Henson for all the good work he did.

---

4) The name "Uncle Tom" has a positive meaning like the character of the man who inspired the novel.

INFERENCES

Based on the article, circle the letter of the best sentence completion.

1) The quick success of Stowe's novel...

a) proves that many people were interested in the plight of the slaves.
b) was only because people had read Josiah Henson's book.
c) only served to hurt Josiah Henson's efforts to help other Black people.
d) was the result of an aggressive advertising campaign.

2) Josiah Henson...

a) was the name of a slave in "Uncle Tom's Cabin."
b) was angry at Harriot Beecher Stowe for using him as the model for her novel.
c) is a positive role model, even today.
d) was a faithful slave.

INTERPRETATION

1) From details in the story or from your own knowledge and experience, can you explain the negative meaning that came to be attached with the name "Uncle Tom"? Why did the term come to be used this way?

2) Did you know that the novel "Uncle Tom's Cabin" is often credited with helping to start the American Civil War? Why do you think the book was so influential? Discuss.

3) Write a short composition about your life story and how you came to Canada, or about how you came to be studying about Canada.

WORD POWER

Circle the letter of the word that means the same as the word on the left.

1) denying	a) classifying	b) injecting	c) disputing
2) inspire	a) influence	b) inform	c) hinder
3) devoting	a) exhausting	b) contributing	c) purchasing
4) adjust	a) integrate	b) diminish	c) return
5) lectured	a) administrated	b) preached	c) interpreted
6) character	a) limitations	b) reverence	c) personality

FIND-THE-WORDS PUZZLE

You will find words from the article hidden in the box below. Find each word and
circle all its letters. To find the words you may have to read from left-to-right,
from right-to-left, upward, downward or diagonally. You should be able to find all
the words given in the list below the box.

F	C	Y	D	E	D	N	U	O	F	I	C
L	A	T	A	U	T	H	O	R	S	N	E
U	F	I	C	T	I	O	N	A	L	H	L
F	L	N	V	A	F	U	V	H	L	A	E
H	O	U	M	W	B	F	E	S	I	B	B
T	B	M	H	C	W	I	L	C	K	I	R
I	M	M	I	G	R	A	N	T	S	T	I
A	Y	O	M	E	V	G	V	C	F	A	T
F	S	C	M	E	R	F	L	E	E	N	Y
D	U	R	R	A	N	O	V	E	L	T	H
W	O	Y	V	R	E	D	N	I	M	E	R
F	R	E	E	D	O	M	E	L	C	N	U

AUTHOR	GRAVE
CABIN	IMMIGRANTS
CELEBRITY	INHABITANT
COMMUNITY	NOVEL
FAITHFUL	REMINDER
FICTIONAL	SKILLS
FORMER	SLAVERY
FLEE	SYMBOL
FOUNDED	UNCLE
FREEDOM	WAVE

ANSWER KEY

THE MAIN IDEA

d) The man who inspired the novel "Uncle Tom's Cabin".

UNDERSTANDING WHAT YOU READ

1) The tiny cabin in Dresden is famous because it is recognized for the fact it was once home to a former slave whose life story helped inspire Harriot Beecher Stowe to write her book, "Uncle Tom's Cabin." It is also famous because it is considered an important symbol of the arrival of early Black immigrants to Canada. And it is considered a lasting reminder of the ongoing struggle for social equality facing many Blacks in North America today, also.
2) It is estimated that as many as fifty-thousand Blacks may have entered Canada in the first half of the 1800s. Most of these new Canadians were escaping slaves who believed that crossing the border meant safety and freedom.
3) The British-American Institute was a trade school for Blacks that offered instruction in such skills as carpentry, smithery, cooking and sewing.
4) "Uncle Tom's Cabin" was a book about the evils of slavery. It detailed the sad life of a faithful Black slave.

REMEMBERING DETAILS

1) T
2) F   In an attempt to raise money for the British-American Institute, Henson decided to publish his life story, called "The Life of Josiah Henson, Formerly A Slave, Now an Inhabitant of Canada."
3) F   Unfortunately, people remember Josiah Henson for the fictional character modeled after him in Harriot Beecher Stowe's book and not for what he truly was.
4) F   The name "Uncle Tom" soon took on a negative meaning far different than the character of the man who inspired it.

INFERENCES

1) a
2) c

WORD POWER

1) c
2) a
3) b
4) a
5) b
6) c

FIND-THE-WORDS PUZZLE

```
      Y D E D N U O F I   C
L     T A U T H O R S N   E
U F I C T I O N A L H     L
F L N   A           L A   E
H O U       B       S I B B
T B M       W I L     K I R
I M M I G R A N T S   T I
A Y O   E V G V       A T
F S C M E R F L E E N Y
  R R A N O V E L T
  O Y V R E D N I M E R
F R E E D O M E L C N U
```

V: Vancouver

1   It is not uncommon to hear visitors to Vancouver praise the city as one of the most beautiful in the world. But when those tourists happen to be the King of England and his daughter, there's reason to believe they might be right.

2   Such was the case when former King George VI toured British Columbia with his daughter, Princess Elizabeth, in 1939. Today, Elizabeth is Queen Elizabeth II. Upon their visit to Vancouver, Her Majesty was heard to say: "This seems to me the place to live." Her words reflect the feelings of millions of people who see the City of Vancouver as a shining jewel in Canada's national crown.

3   Perhaps the most obvious reason for Vancouver's high praise is the city's location. Built on the Burrard Inlet on British Columbia's west coast, Vancouver has one of the most scenic backdrops in all of Canada. On one side there are the snow-crested peaks of the Rocky Mountains. On the other lies the vast waters of the Pacific Ocean. A visitor to Vancouver can wake to an early swim in the ocean, spend the afternoon hiking through the city's extensive parklands, and wind up night-skiing on one of the many surrounding slopes. No other city in Canada can offer such a wide variety of activities to its residents.

4   The history of the area dates back to around 500 BC, when coastal Indians became the first permanent settlers. Although a Spanish naval vessel is

reported to have dropped anchor here in 1791, it was the arrival of Captain George Vancouver of Britain a year later that marked the beginning of European settlement in the area.

5   For the next half-century, however, very little activity took place on the Burrard Peninsula. This finally changed in the 1860s, when a new brickyard and several sawmills began to draw people to the area. Originally known as Granville Townsite, the small settlement officially became the City of Vancouver in 1886.

6   In May of the next year, the Canadian Pacific Railway tracks finally arrived in Vancouver. With the new railway line linking the city to the rest of the country, Vancouver experienced a major boom in business and population. The city's deep natural year-round harbour helped Vancouver grow into Canada's main west coast seaport, while the warm climate and scenic beauty made it a favourite destination for new immigrants to Canada.

7   In 1900, Vancouver's population had grown to just over 100,000 people. Today it ranks 3rd behind Toronto and Montreal on the list of Canada's largest cities. Over 1.3 million people live and work in the metropolitan area of the City of Vancouver.

8   This area includes such attractions as Vancouver's famous Stanley Park. The 1,000 acre wilderness reserve in the heart of the city features a zoo, a public aquarium complete with whales and dolphins, thousands of walking trails, and a stunning view of the city and its harbour.

9   With so many splendid features, it's no wonder Queen Elizabeth named Vancouver the place to be on Canada's west coast.

THE MAIN IDEA

Circle the letter of the sentence which best describes the main idea of the article about Vancouver. Be prepared to support your answer.

a) What royalty thinks of Vancouver.
b) The Vancouver story.
c) Vancouver: A great place to live!
d) The city with variety.

UNDERSTANDING WHAT YOU READ

If you can, answer these questions from memory. If you cannot, look back at the article.

1) What is the most obvious reason for Vancouver to receive such high praise?

_______ ____

2) Who were the first settlers in the area around Vancouver? When?

____

3) What finally drew some people to the Vancouver area in the 1860s?

____

4) What are some of the attractions Vancouver has to offer?

____

REMEMBERING DETAILS

Write TRUE or FALSE under each statement. If the statement is false, write the statement correctly.

1) Tourists seem to find Vancouver very boring.

____

2) Residents of Vancouver find the city boring because there is nothing to do.

____

3) Vancouver's deep natural year-round harbour helped the city grow into a major seaport.

____

4) Vancouver is the largest city in Canada.

_______ ____ V3

INFERENCES

Based on the article, circle the letter of the best sentence completion.

1) Tourists...

a) enjoy praising things.
b) sometimes get lost in Stanley Park.
c) find Vancouver very praiseworthy.
d) flock to see the kings and queens that visit Vancouver.

2) Vancouver really started to grow when...

a) the name was changed from Granville Townsite.
b) industry arrived.
c) the harbour opened.
d) Stanley Park was opened.

INTERPRETATION

1) Which Canadian city would you like to live in the most? Why? Would you
   prefer to live in a big city or a small town? Or would you prefer to live in a
   city somewhere else in the world? Where? Why? Discuss.

2) In the essay the author gives a few examples of things that can be done in a
   single day in Vancouver. Write a short composition and call it My Day in
   Vancouver. In the composition give a description of the kind of day you would
   spend in Vancouver.

3) Vancouver is the 3rd largest city in Canada behind Toronto and Montreal.
   Which cities are the 4th and 5th largest in Canada? What are the five largest
   cities in North America? Five largest in the world?

WORD POWER

Circle the letter of the word that means the same as the word on the left.

1) uncommon	a) immodest	b) regular	c) unusual
2) obvious	a) minute	b) conspicuous	c) grotesque
3) extensive	a) exciting	b) ample	c) complex
4) variety	a) assortment	b) memoir	c) legacy
5) boom	a) decline	b) regulation	c) upswing
6) stunning	a) stifling	b) suffocating	c) breathtaking

FIND-THE-WORDS PUZZLE

You will find words from the article hidden in the box below. Find each word and
circle all its letters. To find the words you may have to read from left-to-right,
from right-to-left, upward, downward or diagonally. You should be able to find all
the words given in the list below the box.

```
T  M  R  J  E  G  N  I  N  I  H  S
E  E  E  B  R  E  I  G  N  I  N  G
Y  T  S  A  J  E  W  E  L  R  A  N
B  R  I  C  K  Y  A  R  D  D  C  I
S  O  D  K  P  R  A  I  S  E  T  D
L  P  E  D  S  T  Y  D  G  V  I  N
L  O  N  R  E  L  R  N  W  A  V  U
I  L  T  O  A  A  I  O  V  S  I  O
M  I  S  P  W  K  R  V  P  T  T  R
W  T  Y  S  N  G  J  C  E  A  I  R
A  A  E  I  M  A  R  K  E  D  E  U
S  N  L  A  T  S  A  O  C  M  S  S
```

ACTIVITIES	METROPOLITAN
BACKDROPS	PRAISE
BRICKYARD	REIGNING
COASTAL	RESIDENTS
DRAW	SAWMILLS
GROW	SEAPORT
JEWEL	SHINING
LINKING	SURROUNDING
LIVE	VAST
MARKED	YET

ANSWER KEY

THE MAIN IDEA

b) The Vancouver story.

UNDERSTANDING WHAT YOU READ

1) The most obvious reason for Vancouver's high praise is the city's location. Built on the Burrard Inlet on British Columbia's west coast, Vancouver has one of the most scenic backdrops in all of Canada. On one side there's the snow-crested peaks of the Rocky Mountains. On the other lies the vast waters of the Pacific Ocean.
2) Coastal Indians became the first permanent settlers in the Vancouver area around 500 BC.
3) The building of a new brickyard and several sawmills began to draw people to the area in the 1860s.
4) Vancouver has attractions like the famous Stanley Park. The 1,000 acre wilderness reserve in the heart of the city features a zoo, a public aquarium complete with whales and dolphins, thousands of walking trails and a stunning view of the city and its harbour.

REMEMBERING DETAILS

1) F   It is not uncommon to hear visitors to Vancouver praise the city as one of the most beautiful in the world.

2)   Vancouver residents do not find their city boring because no other city in Canada can offer such a wide variety of activities.

3) T

4) F   Vancouver ranks 3rd behind Toronto and Montreal on the list of Canada's largest cities.

INFERENCES

1) c
2) b

WORD POWER

1) c
2) b
3) b
4) a
5) c
6) c

FIND-THE-WORDS PUZZLE

T	M	R			G	N	I	N	I	H	S
E	E	E	B	R	E	I	G	N	I	N	G
Y	T	S	A	J	E	W	E	L		A	N
B	R	I	C	K	Y	A	R	D		C	I
S	O	D	K	P	R	A	I	S	E	T	D
L	P	E	D		T		D	G	V	I	N
L	O	N	R		L	R	N	W	A	V	U
I	L	T	O		A	I	O		S	I	O
M	I	S	P	W	K	R	V	P	T	T	R
W	T		S	N	G			E	A	I	R
A	A		I	M	A	R	K	E	D	E	U
S	N	L	A	T	S	A	O	C		S	S

W: Wood Buffalo National Park

1   For thousands of years, the Indians of the Canadian plains relied almost exclusively on the buffalo for their survival. They made pemmican from its meat, fashioned tents and clothing from its hides, and created tools, weapons and jewelry from its bones.

2   As explorers and traders began to push west across the country, the prairies were turned into a killing field for the herds. Millions of buffalo were slaughtered, both for sport and to feed the increasing number of settlers on the prairies. By the late 1800s, the millions of buffalo that once roamed freely on the plains of North America were on the verge of being wiped out forever.

3   Wood Buffalo National Park is a living monument both to the survival of the buffalo and to Canada's vanishing wilderness areas. It was established as a national park in 1922 to provide a permanent home for the world's last remaining herd of wild bison known as the wood buffalo. These bison are larger in size, heavier and darker in colour than a typical plains buffalo. At the time, the government felt that the wood buffalo herd would soon be extinct unless the area was protected.

4   Located on the border between Alberta and the Northwest Territories, Wood Buffalo National Park is not only Canada's largest park, but also the second-largest national park in the world. With nearly 49,000 square kilometres of parkland, Wood Buffalo

covers an area almost as large as Switzerland. Though the park was created to preserve the bison herd, Wood Buffalo has since become known as an important natural habitat for a wide variety of plants, animals and wilderness areas that symbolize the Canadian north.

5   Wood Buffalo National Park is divided into four unique "life zones:" the Caribou and Birch Uplands, the Alberta Plateau. the Slave River Lowlands and the Peace-Athabasca Delta. Within these zones can be found crystal clear streams, shallow lakes and marshes, granite hills and low-lying grasslands. The park also protects 80 percent of one of the world's largest freshwater deltas, the Peace-Athabasca.

6   While the number of buffalo in the park has grown from just 1,500 in 1922 to over 10,000 today, other animals have also benefited by living in the protective environment of Wood Buffalo National Park. The largest density of wolves in North America prowls the region, feeding on the bison herds that roam the park. The endangered peregrine falcon is known to breed here. Even more encouraging was the discovery in 1954 of the last natural nesting ground of the endangered whooping crane. The whooping crane was once almost extinct, but now North America's tallest bird flies north from the Texas wetlands each summer to lay its eggs in the park.

In 1983, after more than 60 years of 7 protecting endangered species, Wood Buffalo National Park was declared a World Heritage Site by the United Nations.

THE MAIN IDEA

Circle the letter of the sentence which best describes the main idea of the article about Wood Buffalo National Park. Be prepared to support your answer.

a) A park created to preserve a species.
b) Things that can be made from buffalo.
c) A government decision.
d) Endangered species.

UNDERSTANDING WHAT YOU READ

If you can, answer these questions from memory. If you cannot, look back at the article.

1) By the late 1800s, what had happened to the buffalo herds?

____

2) Where is Wood Buffalo National Park located?

____

3) What other endangered species can be found in the park?

____

4) What happened to the Wood Buffalo National Park in 1983?

____

REMEMBERING DETAILS

Write TRUE or FALSE under each statement. If the statement is false, write the statement correctly.

1) Indians of the Canadian plains paid no attention to the buffalo.

____

2) Wood buffalo are smaller, lighter in colour and weigh less than a typical plains buffalo.

____

3) Wood Buffalo National Park is only known for being a natural habitat for buffalo.

____

4) Whooping cranes have been known to lay their eggs in Wood Buffalo National Park.

____

INFERENCES

Based on the article, circle the letter of the best sentence completion.

1) The Canadian government...

a) should have done more.
b) saved the wood buffalo from becoming extinct.
c) purposely set out to rescue the whooping crane.
d) cannot figure out how to stop the wolves from attacking the buffalo.

2) The Plains Indians...

a) made good use of each buffalo they killed.
b) were in favour of the creation of the park.
c) were living on the territory which would become the park.
d) understood the slaughter of the buffalo.

INTERPRETATION

1) Many of the buffalo killed on the Canadian plains were killed for sport. In many cases the buffalo was simply left were it was shot, with not even its meat being taken. Do you think the hunting of wild animals, such as moose and deer. should be permitted? Why? Under what circumstances? Why not?

2) Write the script of a conversation between a Plains Indian and a recently arrived settler. Have the Native person explain the value of the buffalo, while the settler explains the sport of shooting buffalo.

3) Write a short composition about an endangered species. Your local library should have the information. You may want to describe any efforts being made to protect that species. Discuss.

WORD POWER

Circle the letter of the word that means the same as the word on the left.

1) relied	a) tolerated	b) conceived	c) depended
2) verge	a) outside	b) brink	c) disaster
3) benefited	a) gained	b) grown	c) lessened
4) density	a) crux	b) concentration	c) dynasty
5) breed	a) rest	b) live	c) reproduce
6) species	a) friends	b) types	c) subjects

FIND-THE-WORDS PUZZLE

You will find words from the article hidden in the box below. Find each word and circle all its letters. To find the words you may have to read from left-to-right, from right-to-left, upward, downward or diagonally. You should be able to find all the words given in the list below the box.

```
N  H  E  R  D  N  O  S  I  B  G  S
E  L  A  Y  R  O  A  M  F  N  E  R
S  L  H  B  L  Y  T  H  I  N  S  Y
T  A  I  K  I  O  B  H  O  G  E  D
I  T  D  E  O  T  S  B  O  Z  R  E
N  S  E  L  U  I  A  N  L  E  T  N
G  Y  S  L  N  Q  E  T  A  T  E  O
N  R  B  A  O  N  I  H  F  I  M  I
O  C  V  M  A  F  B  N  F  N  O  H
B  D  E  R  E  T  H  G  U  A  L  S
O  C  C  Z  O  N  E  S  B  R  I  A
P  R  E  S  E  R  V  E  C  G  K  F
```

BISON	KILOMETRES
BONES	LAY
BUFFALO	NESTING
CRANE	PRESERVE
CRYSTAL	ROAM
FASHIONED	SLAUGHTERED
GRANITE	TOOLS
HABITAT	UNIQUE
HERD	VANISHING
HIDES	ZONES

ANSWER KEY

THE MAIN IDEA

a) A park created to preserve a species.

UNDERSTANDING WHAT YOU READ

1) By the late 1800s, the millions of buffalo that once roamed freely on the plains of North America were on the verge of being wiped out forever.
2) Wood Buffalo National Park is located on the border between Alberta and the Northwest Territories.
3) Other endangered species that have been found in the park include peregrine falcons and whooping cranes.
4) In 1983, after more than 60 years of protecting endangered species, Wood Buffalo National Park was declared a World Heritage Site by the United Nations.

REMEMBERING DETAILS

1) F   For thousands of years, the Indians of the Canadian plains relied almost exclusively on the buffalo for their survival. They made pemmican from its meat, fashioned tents and clothing from its hides, and created tools, weapons and jewelry from its bones.
2) F   Wood buffalo are larger in size, heavier and darker in colour than a typical plains buffalo.
3) F   Wood Buffalo is also known as an important natural habitat for a wide variety of plants, animals and wilderness areas that symbolize the Canadian north.
4) T

INFERENCES

1) b
2) a

WORD POWER

1) c
2) b
3) a
4) b
5) c
6) b

FIND-THE-WORDS PUZZLE

N	H	E	R	D	N	O	S	I	B	G	S
E	L	A	Y	R	O	A	M		N	E	
S	L	H	B			T		I	N	S	
T	A	I		I	O		H	O		E	D
I	T	D	E	O	T	S	B	O		R	E
N	S	E	L	U	I	A		L	E	T	N
G	Y	S		N	Q	E	T	A	T	E	O
	R		A		N	I		F	I	M	I
	C	V		A			N	F	N	O	H
	D	E	R	E	T	H	G	U	A	L	S
		C	Z	O	N	E	S	B	R	I	A
P	R	E	S	E	R	V	E		G	K	F

X: XOE OTO

1   Thanks to the nationwide services of Canada Post, you can mail a letter anywhere in the country. Address your letter with the postal code XOE OTO, however, and it can only be headed for one destination: Inuvik, Northwest Territories.

2   Sitting some 200 kilometres above the Arctic Circle, Inuvik is one of the northernmost settlements in Canada. But the cold dark winters that blanket this tiny community have not stopped Inuvik from becoming one of the most unique and colourful towns in the Western Arctic region.

3   Inuvik is located at the northern end of the Dempster Highway in the delta region of the Mackenzie River. This is the farthest north you can drive on a public highway on the continent. Beginning in the Yukon at Dawson City, the Dempster Highway travels 681 kilometres, winding its way north through mountains and across the Arctic Circle until it reaches Inuvik.

4   Many people imagine Arctic communities to be nothing more than snow-covered log cabins, fishing huts or igloos. Fortunately, Inuvik offers much more to its mix of Inuit, Dene and English-speaking residents. In fact, the town is the first successful "scientifically planned" community in Canada.

5   It was designed as a substitute for the nearby town of Aklivik. When river

erosion and unstable soil caused
Aklivik to start sinking into the Delta,
the government decided to replace it by
building Inuvik, the area's first modern
community offering the same features
and services as a typical Canadian
town.

6   Though construction on Inuvik began
in 1954, it was not an easy task.
Building in the Arctic meant
overcoming permafrost, a condition
that caused the ground to stay frozen
all year long. Planners had to develop
ways to make sure buildings would
remain safe. As a result, many of
Inuvik's buildings were constructed on
stilts.

7   These stilts -- or legs -- were driven
nearly 20 feet into the frozen ground.
Buildings were then erected on the
stilts in order to keep the heat inside
from melting the ground and causing
the buildings to shift or collapse.
Metal tunnels called utilidors were also

part of the design. These tunnels
housed all the pipes and wires for
heating, water service and electricity.
To complete the unique look of the
town, most of the buildings were
painted bright pastel colours, a stark
contrast to the natural colours of the
Arctic wilderness.

Inuvik quickly became the   8
government and transportation centre
for the entire region. During the '70s',
it became the supply base for oil and
gas exploration activities north of the
Arctic Circle. The result was a decade
of prosperity for the over 3,000
residents of the town.

While Inuvik still serves as a model   9
for urban planning in the north, it is the
shared sense of community that gives
this cold northern town its warm feel.
That's one of the reasons why people
from many different cultures list their
home address as Inuvik, XOE OTO.

THE MAIN IDEA

Circle the letter of the sentence which best describes the main idea of the article
about Inuvik. Be prepared to support your answer.

a) The postal code of Inuvik.
b) A city of log cabins, fishing huts and igloos.
c) The first scientifically planned community in Canada.
d) The end of the Dempster Highway.

UNDERSTANDING WHAT YOU READ

If you can, answer these questions from memory. If you cannot, look back at the article.

1) Where is Inuvik located?

____

2) Why did Inuvik come to exist?

____

3) Why are the buildings on stilts?

____

4) How many people live in Inuvik?

____

REMEMBERING DETAILS

Write TRUE or FALSE under each statement. If the statement is false, write the statement correctly.

1) The Dempster Highway runs 850 kilometres from Vancouver to Whitehorse.

____

2) Building Inuvik was an easy task because there were no obstacles for construction crews to overcome.

____

3) During the '70s', Inuvik was the base for gold mining operations in the north.

____

4) It is the shared sense of community that gives Inuvik its warm feel.

____

INFERENCES

Based on the article, circle the letter of the best sentence completion.

1) Many people...

a) visit Inuvik.
b) have car trouble on the Dempster Highway.
c) would find living in a house on stilts very odd.
d) have the wrong impression as to what life is like in an Arctic community.

2) Even though Inuvik is so far north...

a) tourists can always be found walking the streets.
b) it is still a friendly place because the residents have warm hearts.
c) summers are warm and pleasant.
d) residents find it easy to heat their homes because oil and gas are found nearby.

INTERPRETATION

1) If given the opportunity, would you live in Inuvik? Why would you?
   Why wouldn't you? Would life be better or worse in Inuvik than where you
   are living today? Discuss.

2) Using your own knowledge or from doing research, write a paragraph or two
   on one aspect of life in the Arctic for the Inuit. Topics can include
   transportation, art, religion, history, way of life, clothing, social organization,
   diet, housing or another topic of your choice.

3) If given your choice, in what type of a climate would you prefer to live? A
   cold place? A hot place? Or some place with cold winters and hot summers?
   What factors influence your decision? Discuss.

WORD POWER

Circle the letter of the word that means the same as the word on the left.

1) blanket	a) bother	b) cover	c) challenge
2) substitute	a) addition	b) match	c) replacement
3) erosion	a) deterioration	b) levels	c) soot
4) shift	a) vibrate	b) move	c) tumble
5) housed	a) scuttled	b) concealed	c) singed
6) decade	a) extended period	b) a while	c) ten years

FIND-THE-WORDS PUZZLE

You will find words from the article hidden in the box below. Find each word and
circle all its letters. To find the words you may have to read from left-to-right,
from right-to-left, upward, downward or diagonally. You should be able to find all
the words given in the list below the box.

```
H  C  O  N  T  I  N  E  N  T  Y  P
E  U  Q  I  N  U  H  U  T  S  D  W
D  P  E  R  M  A  F  R  O  S  T  I
I  G  L  O  O  S  F  C  A  D  I  N
W  A  R  M  Z  U  F  R  P  E  U  D
N  U  R  B  A  N  T  D  O  Q  N  I
O  E  S  N  E  S  E  L  L  Z  I  N
I  Q  W  F  A  T  P  K  U  G  E  G
T  Y  P  I  C  A  L  Z  R  S  I  N
A  D  G  E  Q  B  W  G  T  A  E  H
N  N  R  D  E  L  T  A  F  E  T  R
I  E  O  R  F  E  S  T  L  I  T  S
```

CONTINENT	RESULT
DELTA	SENSE
ERECTED	STARK
FROZEN	STILTS
HEAT	TYPICAL
HUTS	UNIQUE
IGLOOS	UNSTABLE
INUIT	URBAN
NATIONWIDE	WARM
PERMAFROST	WINDING

ANSWER KEY

THE MAIN IDEA

c) The first scientifically planned community in Canada.

UNDERSTANDING WHAT YOU READ

1) Inuvik is located at the northern end of the Dempster Highway in the delta region of the Mackenzie River. Inuvik is one of the northernmost settlements in Canada.   It is 200 kilometres above the Arctic Circle,
2) Inuvik was designed as a substitute for the nearby town of Aklivik. When river erosion and unstable soil caused Aklivik to start sinking into the Delta, the government decided to replace it by building Inuvik.
3) Buildings were erected on stilts in order to keep the heat inside from melting the ground and causing the buildings to shift or collapse.
4) Over 3,000 people live in Inuvik.

REMEMBERING DETAILS

1) F   The Dempster Highway travels 681 kilometres from Dawson City to Inuvik.
2) F   Building Inuvik was not an easy task. The obstacle construction crews had to overcome was permafrost, a condition that caused the ground to stay frozen all year long.
3) F   During the '70s', Inuvik was the supply base for oil and gas exploration activities north of the Arctic Circle.
4) T

INFERENCES

1) d
2) b

WORD POWER

1) b
2) c
3) a
4) b
5) b
6) c

FIND-THE-WORDS PUZZLE

```
    C   O   N   T   I   N   E   N   T
E   U   Q   I   N   U   H   U   T   S           W
D   P   E   R   M   A   F   R   O   S   T       I
I   G   L   O   O   S   F               I   N
W   A   R   M       U       R           U   D
N   U   R   B   A   N   T   D   O       N   I
O   E   S   N   E   S   E   L       Z   I   N
I               T       K   U       E   G
T   Y   P   I   C   A   L       R   S       N
A           E       B           T   A   E   H
N       R   D   E   L   T   A           T   R
    E               E   S   T   L   I   T   S
```

Y: Yukon Territory

1   In February, 1947, the coldest temperature ever recorded in Canada was registered at Snag Airport in the Yukon Territory, close to the Alaskan border. That day the thermometer read minus   63 degrees Celcius.

2   This image of a frozen wilderness is evoked for many people by the Yukon Territory. As the most North-Western part of Canada, the Yukon is often thought to be nothing more than a barren landscape known for its short summers and ice cold winters. But a closer look at life in the Yukon reveals a rugged land of incredible beauty, featuring snow-fed lakes, white-capped mountains, and forests and streams alive with a variety of wildlife.

3   The territory gets its name from the Loucheux Indians, who used the word "Yu-Kun-Ah," meaning "great river," to describe the Yukon River. At 3,185 kilometres long, the mighty Yukon River is the fifth longest river in all of North America. Nearly 1,150 kilometres of the river flow within Yukon Territory boundaries.

4   The Yukon River has been at the centre of much of the history, exploration and development of the area. Russian travellers sailing the river in the 1830s were amongst the first non-Native people to explore the region. In the 1840s, fur-trappers working for the Hudson's Bay Company explored many new routes by travelling inland up the river. This lead to settlements in areas like Fort Selkirk and Herschel Island.

5   The discovery of gold in the Yukon Territory proved to be the most important event in the history of the area. On August 17, 1896, the world's greatest gold rush began when gold ore was found in Bonanza Creek near the Klondike River. Over 40,000 adventurers quickly made their way to the Yukon in search of gold-lined streams, and in one month Dawson City grew into the biggest city west of Winnipeg.

6   On June 13, 1898, the Yukon Territory became a part of Canada, with Dawson City being named its capital. However, when the gold-rush ended in 1904, so did the rush of people into Dawson City. Soon other mining towns were rising up across the Yukon. When the Alaska Highway was built during World War II, it opened the Yukon to further development, and the population of Dawson City continued to decline. In 1953, the capital city was changed from Dawson to Whitehorse.

7   Today tourism is the Yukon's newest "goldmine," as people travel north to enjoy the spectacular scenery of the area. One of the most popular tourist destinations is Kluane National Park. Located in the Southwest Yukon, Kluane includes Canada's highest mountain, Mount Logan. It stands 5,591 metres high. The Yukon also features North America's largest population of grizzly bears, plus moose, black bears, and caribou.

8   In fact, animals far outnumber humans in the Yukon. Despite being 8th overall in size, the Yukon Territory ranks last in Canada's population With just over 24,000 people, the Yukon remains a true part of the Canadian wilderness.

THE MAIN IDEA

Circle the letter of the sentence which best describes the main idea of the article about the Yukon Territory. Be prepared to support your answer.

a) The coldest place in Canada.
b) The decline of Dawson City.
c) The Yukon Territory.
d) The discovery of gold in the Yukon.

UNDERSTANDING WHAT YOU READ

If you can, answer these questions from memory. If you cannot, look back at the article.

1) Where was the coldest temperature in Canada recorded? What was the temperature?

____

2) What lead to settlements in areas like Fort Selkirk and Herschel Island?

____

3) Why did over 40,000 adventurers rush to the Yukon?

____

4) What is one of the Yukon Territory's most popular tourist destinations? Where is it located?

____

REMEMBERING DETAILS

Write TRUE or FALSE under each statement. If the statement is false, write the statement correctly.

1) The Yukon is a rugged land of incredible beauty, featuring snow-fed lakes, white-capped mountains, and forests and streams with a variety of wildlife.

____ ____

2) The discovery of gold did not much effect the Yukon Territory.

____

3) When the Alaska Highway was built in 1970, it helped the population of Dawson City grow.

____

4) The Yukon has North America's largest population of kangaroos, crocodiles and panda bears.

____

INFERENCES

Based on the article, circle the letter of the best sentence completion.

1) The fur trade...

a) lasted a shorter length of time than the gold rush did.
b) was more important in eastern Canada.
c) helped create new towns in the Yukon Territory.
d) brought the first non-Natives to the Yukon.

2) When hiking through the Yukon Territory wilderness...

a) you are more likely to meet animals rather than people.
b) one should bring one's fishing rod and rifle.
c) you should follow the old fur-trapper trails.
d) bring a compass.

INTERPRETATION

1) The Yukon Territory sounds like a great place to go camping. Have you ever
   been camping? If "Yes," was it in the wilderness? Describe your trip. If
   "No," why not? Do you like camping? Why? Why not? Discuss.

2) Write a short composition about being lost for twenty-four hours in the Yukon
   wilderness.

3) Write the script of a conversation between any two people of your choice
   during the gold rush in the Yukon. Perform your role plays for the rest of the
   class.

WORD POWER

Circle the letter of the word that means the same as the word on the left.

1) recorded	a) experienced	b) detonated	c) spoken
2) alive	a) selecting	b) teeming	c) tight
3) lead	a) projected	b) bought	c) influenced
4) rush	a) cramp	b) wave	c) nest
5) changed	a) switched	b) reversed	c) negated
6) ranks	a) stays	b) mobilizes	c) measures

FIND-THE-WORDS PUZZLE

You will find words from the article hidden in the box below. Find each word and circle all its letters. To find the words you may have to read from left-to-right, from right-to-left, upward, downward or diagonally. You should be able to find all the words given in the list below the box.

```
V  L  A  N  D  S  C  A  P  E  E  G
H  G  I  H  C  E  L  C  I  U  S  O
D  Y  U  S  L  A  E  V  E  R  O  L
H  L  F  E  A  T  U  R  E  S  O  H
A  M  O  N  G  S  T  B  P  M  M  I
L  G  M  G  A  S  M  A  E  R  T  S
A  C  N  I  S  U  Y  U  K  O  N  T
T  S  S  E  N  R  E  D  L  I  W  O
I  E  A  T  Y  I  A  P  A  R  T  R
P  L  U  U  L  T  N  E  V  E  G  Y
A  O  R  E  V  I  R  G  B  Y  H  B
C  P  O  P  U  L  A  T  I  O  N  O
```

AMONGST	MINING
BEARS	MOOSE
CAPITAL	OUTNUMBER
CELCIUS	PART
EVENT	POPULATION
FEATURES	REVEALS
GOLD	RIVER
HISTORY	STREAMS
HIGH	WILDERNESS
LANDSCAPE	YUKON

ANSWER KEY

THE MAIN IDEA

c) The Yukon Territory.

UNDERSTANDING WHAT YOU READ

1) The coldest temperature ever recorded in Canada was registered at Snag Airport in the Yukon Territory, close to the Alaskan border. That day the thermometer read minus 63 degrees Celcius.
2) Settlements in areas like Fort Selkirk and Herschel Island began after fur-trappers working for the Hudson's Bay Company explored many new routes through the Yukon wilderness.
3) Over 40,000 adventurers quickly made their way to the Yukon in search of gold-lined streams.
4) One of the Yukon's most popular tourist destinations is Kluane National Park. It is located in the Southwest Yukon.

REMEMBERING DETAILS

1) T
2) F   The discovery of gold in the Yukon proved to be the most important event in the history of the area.
3) F   When the Alaska Highway was built during World War II, it opened the Yukon to further development, and the population of Dawson City continued to decline.
4) F   The Yukon has North America's largest population of grizzly bears, plus moose, black bears, and caribou.

INFERENCES

1) c
2) a

WORD POWER

1) a
2) b
3) c
4) b
5) a
6) c

FIND-THE-WORDS PUZZLE

	L	A	N	D	S	C	A	P	E	E	
H	G	I	H	C	E	L	C	I	U	S	
D			S	L	A	E	V	E	R	O	
	L	F	E	A	T	U	R	E	S	O	H
A	M	O	N	G	S	T	B			M	I
L		M	G		S	M	A	E	R	T	S
A			I	S	U	Y	U	K	O	N	T
T	S	S	E	N	R	E	D	L	I	W	O
I			T		I	A	P	A	R	T	R
P		U			T	N	E	V	E		Y
A	O	R	E	V	I	R	G	B			
C	P	O	P	U	L	A	T	I	O	N	

Z: Zoos

1   Walking through the thick forests of the Canadian wilderness, there is a good chance you might see a moose, a deer, a beaver or even a bear. These are just a few of the hundreds of species that roam wild in Canada's countryside from coast to coast. If you're more interested in zebras, hyenas and rhinos, however, the only place in Canada you're likely to find them is at a zoo.

2   Throughout the centuries humans have been fascinated by the living creatures that share the earth. This curiosity has helped make zoos one of the most popular attractions in the world. In North America alone, over 100 million people visit zoos each year. This tradition dates back to the ancient empires of China, Greece, Egypt and Rome, when exotic animals were often imported to such countries from around the world. These animals were often kept as pets, used for worship, or put on public display.

3   One of the important factors that determines what kinds of animals can live in certain parts of the world is climate. In Canada, bitterly cold winters make it impossible for certain species to survive outside. As a result, zoos provide Canadians with the opportunity to observe animals that wouldn't normally be found in Canada.

4   There are many different kinds of zoos. In Canada, they include everything from aquariums that specialize in marine mammals and fish, to theme parks full of wild jungle

cats, gorillas, hippos and other exotic animals.

5   By far the largest zoo in Canada is the Metropolitan Toronto Zoo, which opened in 1974. Built on 710 acres of land in the city's east end, the Toronto Zoo is considered one of the Top 10 in the world. It also has one of the largest animal populations in North America, with more than 4,000 animals from over 800 different species living within the zoo's boundaries.

6   One of the unique features of the Toronto Zoo is that animals are grouped together according to where they live in the wild. Special sections feature animals from such places as Africa, Australia, the Polar regions and South America. The zoo also has a pavilion designed to hold the largest elephant herd in Canada. Most of the zoo's animals can be seen year-round thanks to its modern "indoor" design.

7   Several other Canadian provinces also have impressive zoos. The Vancouver Aquarium is well known for its collection of marine mammals and fish. The Calgary Zoo features a Polar Bear complex complete with bears, seals, beavers and otters, plus a Pre-historic Park with over 20 life-size dinosaurs. In Manitoba, the Assiniboine Park Zoo houses several endangered species. The St-Felicien Zoological Park in Quebec has over 2,400 animals from around the world, while Salmonier Nature Park in Newfoundland keeps only those species found in Newfoundland and Labrador.

8   Some people argue that zoos are simply prisons for animals used to roaming free. For many endangered species, however, Canada's zoos provide the best chance for survival in a world where wilderness is rapidly disappearing.

THE MAIN IDEA

Circle the letter of the sentence which best describes the main idea of the article about Zoos. Be prepared to support your answer.

a) The history of exotic animals.
b) The importance of climate.
c) The many zoos of Canada.
d) Zoos which protect endangered species.

UNDERSTANDING WHAT YOU READ

If you can, answer these questions from memory. If you cannot, look back at the article.

1) Name a few of the hundreds of species that roam wild in Canada?

---

2) With what do zoos provide Canadians?

---

3) How many animals are housed at the Toronto Zoo? From how many species?

---

4) What is the policy of the Salmonier Nature Park in Newfoundland?

REMEMBERING DETAILS

Write TRUE or FALSE under each statement. If the statement is false, write the statement correctly.

1) Zoos are a recent invention.

---

2) One of the important factors that determines what kinds of animals live in certain parts of the world is climate.

---

3) The Toronto Zoo is big, but it is nothing special.

---

4) Everyone agrees that zoos are a good thing.

INFERENCES

Based on the article, circle the letter of the best sentence completion.

1) Zebras, elephants and rhinos...

a) are native to Africa.
b) are occasionally encountered roaming wild in Canada.
c) could not survive a Canadian winter outside.
d) were worshiped in ancient times.

2) Zoos are not only a place for people to see exotic animals,...

a) they are also a place for people to go and worship.
b) they are also a place for people to argue.
c) they are also a place for some endangered species to live safely.
d) they are also a place to experience different climates.

INTERPRETATION

1) Have you ever been to a zoo in Canada? Where? When? What kinds of
   animals did you see? Have you been to any zoos elsewhere? Discuss.

2) Some people argue that zoos are prisons for animals. Do you agree?
   Disagree? What are your reasons? Discuss.

3) Choose an animal that you would find in a typical Canadian zoo. Write a short
   composition about a day in the life of that animal at the zoo.

WORD POWER

Circle the letter of the word that means the same as the word on the left.

1) roam	a) prey	b) charge	c) walk
2) exotic	a) crazy	b) unfamiliar	c) ferocious
3) marine	a) sea	b) flying	c) cold-blooded
4) impressive	a) outstanding	b) large	c) public
5) collection	a) kennel	b) school	c) assembly
6) found	a) central	b) located	c) imported

FIND-THE-WORDS PUZZLE

You will find words from the article hidden in the box below. Find each word and circle all its letters. To find the words you may have to read from left-to-right, from right-to-left, upward, downward or diagonally. You should be able to find all the words given in the list below the box.

```
B   O   U   N   D   A   R   I   E   S   N   W
P   S   S   E   I   X   S   E   S   U   O   H
E   P   E   A   N   I   M   A   L   S   R   D
T   E   R   F   O   I   T   M   S   E   M   C
S   C   I   R   S   S   R   M   H   R   A   N
N   I   P   E   A   X   U   A   S   C   L   O
O   E   M   E   U   I   B   N   M   A   L   I
S   S   E   N   R   E   D   L   I   W   Y   L
I   P   Q   A   S   P   E   C   I   A   L   I
R   P   U   C   O   M   P   L   E   X   B   V
P   Q   A   W   E   T   A   M   I   L   C   A
A   F   A   S   C   I   N   A   T   E   D   P
```

ACRES	FREE
ANIMALS	HOUSES
AQUARIUMS	MARINE
BOUNDARIES	NORMALLY
CLIMATE	PAVILION
COMPLEX	PETS
DINOSAURS	PRISONS
EAST	SPECIAL
EMPIRES	SPECIES
FASCINATED	WILDERNESS

ANSWER KEY

THE MAIN IDEA

c) The many zoos of Canada.

UNDERSTANDING WHAT YOU READ

1) A few of the hundreds of species that roam wild in Canada are moose, deer, beaver and bear.
2) Zoos provide Canadians with the opportunity to observe animals that wouldn't normally be found in Canada.
3) More than 4,000 animals from over 800 different species are housed at the Toronto Zoo.
4) Salmonier Nature Park in Newfoundland has a policy of keeping only those species found in Newfoundland and Labrador.

REMEMBERING DETAILS

1) F   The tradition of keeping exotic animals for display dates back to the ancient empires of China, Greece, Egypt and Rome.
2) T
3) F   The Toronto Zoo is considered one of the Top 10 in the world. It also has one of the largest animal populations in North America.
4) F   Some people argue that zoos are simply prisons for animals used to roaming free.

INFERENCES

1) c
2) c

WORD POWER

1) c
2) b
3) a
4) a
5) c
6) b

FIND-THE-WORDS PUZZLE

```
B  O  U  N  D  A  R  I  E  S  N
P  S  S  E  I     S  E  S  U  O  H
E  P  E  A  N  I  M  A  L  S  R
T  E  R  F  O  I  T     S  E  M
S  C  I  R  S  S  R  M     R  A  N
N  I  P  E  A     U  A     C  L  O
O  E  M  E  U  I        M  A  L  I
S  S  E  N  R  E  D  L  I  W  Y  L
I        A  S  P  E  C  I  A  L  I
R     U  C  O  M  P  L  E  X     V
P  Q        E  T  A  M  I  L  C  A
A  F  A  S  C  I  N  A  T  E  D  P
```

Made in the USA
Monee, IL
07 July 2026

56544283R00092